String of pearls

String of pearls

Aspects of
God's Word in Psalm 119

Richard Brooks

 EVANGELICAL PRESS

EVANGELICAL PRESS
12 Wooler Street, Darlington, Co. Durham, DL1 1RQ, England.

© Evangelical Press 1990
First published 1990

British Library Cataloguing in Publication Data available.

ISBN 0-85234-280-2

Unless otherwise indicated, Scripture quotations in this publication are from the Holy Bible, New International Version. Copyright © 1973, 1978, 1984 International Bible Society. Published by Hodder & Stoughton.

Cover picture reproduced by courtesy of George Thomson

Typeset by Outset Studios, Hartlepool.
Printed in Great Britain at The Bath Press, Avon.

Thy Word is like a garden, Lord,
With flowers bright and fair;
And everyone who seeks may pluck
A lovely garland there.

Thy Word is like a deep, deep mine;
And jewels rich and rare
Are hidden in its mighty depths,
For every searcher there.

Thy Word is like an armoury,
Where soldiers may repair,
And find for life's long battle-day
All needful weapons there.

Oh, may I love Thy precious Word,
May I explore the mine,
May I its fragrant flowers glean,
May light upon me shine!

Oh, may I find my armour there,
Thy Word my trusty sword;
I'll learn to fight with every foe
The battle of the Lord.

Edwin Hodder (1837-1904).

Contents

Introducing Psalm 119

The most famous characteristic of Psalm 119 is probably that it is the longest psalm in the book of Psalms, extending to no less than 176 verses!

All manner of lavish descriptions have been given of it. Here are some of them:

1. The golden alphabet of the Bible.
2. Twenty-two pearls upon one string.
3. A holy alphabet — so plain that children may understand it, so rich and instructive that the wisest and most experienced may every day learn something from it.
4. The Christian's ABC of the praise, love, power and use of the Word of God.
5. A little Bible, the Scriptures condensed, a mass of bibline, Holy Writ, rewritten in holy emotions and actions.
6. The alphabet of divine love, the paradise of all the doctrines, the storehouse of the Holy Spirit, the school of truth.
7. A pearl island — a garden of sweet flowers.

This psalm has always been exceedingly precious to Christians. One servant of God, Henry Venn, wrote in a letter, 'This is the psalm I have often had recourse to when I could find no spirit of prayer in my own heart, and at length the fire was kindled and I could pray.'

Many references to this psalm are found in the journals of the missionary Henry Martyn. Here is one of them: 'Found some devotion in learning some of the 119th psalm . . . in the evening grew better by reading Psalm 119, which generally brings me into a spiritual frame of mind.'

This little book that I have written is not a verse-by-verse commentary on this great psalm. There are several fine and full commentaries already available, and I would particularly recommend Charles Bridges' verse-by-verse treatment, and C. H. Spurgeon's handling of it in his *Treasury of David*. My purpose in writing is far more modest, though, I trust, worthwhile. I want to introduce the psalm to those who may not yet be familiar with it, to provide a way into it, to whet our appetites with something of the view which it gives of the many facets of the Word of God, and perhaps, even, to supply a starting-point for regular daily meditation upon the psalm. In his account of the life and death of his father Philip, Matthew Henry tells us that 'Once, pressing the study of the Scriptures, he advised us to take a verse of this psalm every morning to meditate upon, and so go over the psalm twice in the year; and that, saith he, will bring you to be in love with all the rest of the Scriptures. He often said, "All grace grows as love to the Word of God grows."'

Before we come to the actual text of Psalm 119, it will be worth our while to take an overall look at the subject, the style and the spirit of this passage of Scripture.

1. The subject of the psalm

If, in a psalm of this length, you found that one thing in particular was mentioned in every single verse, with only one or two exceptions, you could safely assume that this thing was the theme or subject of the psalm. And so it is here. The psalm is concerned with the Word of God and, like a precious jewel, it displays the many facets, lights and aspects of that Word. It has been well said that this psalm is a prolonged meditation upon the excellence of God's Word and its effects, and the strength and happiness it gives to those upon whose hearts it is engraved. It is Scripture commenting upon Scripture; it is the Word telling us about the Word. And in a day when the true doctrine of Scripture is under so much attack (even though it can fend quite well for itself!) how important it is that we take our views of God's Word actually from God's Word itself!

William Cowper remarks that every verse of the psalm

contains in it either a *praise* of God's Word because of some excellent quality which it possesses (e.g. vv. 129,75), an *expression* (Cowper's word is 'protestation') of the psalmist's genuine affection for God's Word (e.g. vv. 97, 24), or a *prayer* for grace that he might be all the more conformed to God's Word (e.g. vv. 9,133).

It is important to observe at this stage that altogether ten different words are used by the psalmist to refer to the Word of God — a fact which, in itself, is a remarkable testimony to the many facets of the Word. Each of these words has its own shade of meaning.

1. God's law. It is given by Him, enacted by Him, derived from Him and is to be our sole rule of conduct.
2. God's way. It declares how He rules, what He purposes and how we should walk before Him.
3. God's testimonies. It witnesses to Him and is attested by Him.
4. God's commandments. It is given with His authority, for our unqualified obedience, not offered on a 'take it or leave it' basis.
5. God's precepts. The word means something which has been placed in trust, or entrusted.
6. God's Word. The living God has spoken and continues to speak in and through His Word.
7. God's judgements. It has been framed in infinite wisdom, and constitutes the holy and true standard by which we shall all be judged.
8. God's righteousness. It is all holy, just and good, and sets forth His rule and his standard of righteousness.
9. God's statutes. His Word is fixed, determined and abiding (the root from which this word comes means 'engraved' or 'inscribed').
10. God's truth/faithfulness. Because He is true and faithful, so is His Word.

2. The style of the psalm

This psalm is written and structured in a particular way. Indeed the different styles in which, God, by His Holy Spirit, has caused Scripture to be written contribute in no small way to the attractiveness and beauty and variety of the Word. As a result we have, over the Bible as a whole, historical narrative, poetry, doctrinal instruction with close arguments, parables, literal language, symbolic language, and so on.

The style, or construction, of Psalm 119 is most beautiful. The 176 verses are divided into twenty-two sections, each eight verses in length. This division corresponds with the number of letters in the Hebrew alphabet (twenty-two) and all the verses in each section begin with the same letter of the alphabet. To describe this in terms of our alphabet, it would mean that verses 1-8 all began with the letter A, verses 9-16 with the letter B, verses 17-24 with the letter C, and so on.

The glory of it all, moreover, is that the psalm is nowhere nearly as repetitive as we might expect from such a structure! Each of the twenty-two sections sets forth some particular facet of God's Word, and as we go through the psalm I shall try to identify the key theme of each section, or one of them, and to remark a little upon it in the hope that this will encourage you to further study and meditation of God's Word for yourself. This book, I say again, is only meant to be a starter!

The following outline of the psalm summarizes these key themes and demonstrates the full, fresh, rich and varied way in which the psalmist treats the doctrine of Scripture:

1. Walking according to God's Word   (1-8)
2. Holiness and God's Word   (9-16)
3. Eyes opened to God's Word   (17-24)
4. The reviving effects of God's Word   (25-32)
5. Dependence upon God's Word   (33-40)
6. The liberty of God's Word   (41-48)
7. People of God's Word   (49-56)
8. God as the portion of those who obey His Word   (57-64)
9. Affliction and God's Word   (65-72)
10. Prayer stirred up by God's Word   (73-80)
11. The comfort of God's Word   (81-88)
12. The firmness of God's Word   (89-96)
13. Loving God's Word   (97-104)
14. The illumination of God's Word   (105-112)
15. God as the sustainer and upholder of those who
    love His Word   (113-120)

16. A plea to the God of the Word to act   (121-128)
17. The wonderful character of God's Word   (129-136)
18. The righteousness of God's Word   (137-144)
19. The Word and prayer   (145-152)
20. The God of the Word   (153-160)
21. The believer's response to God's Word   (161-168)
22. The straying sheep returning to God's Word   (169-176)

3. The spirit of the psalm

The Word of God lives and breathes; it is not a dead letter. Psalm 119 breathes a warm, devotional and practical spirit all the way through.

Jonathan Edwards says, 'I know of no part of the Holy Scriptures where the nature and evidences of true and sincere godliness are so fully and largely insisted upon and set out as in the 119th psalm . . . The excellency of holiness is represented as the immediate object of a spiritual taste and delight.'

And Charles Bridges says of this psalm, 'It may be considered as the journal of one who was deeply taught in the things of God and long practised in the life and walk of faith. It contains the anatomy of experimental [that is, practical, spiritual, godly, true] religion . . . It is given for the use of believers in all ages as an excellent touchstone of vital godliness . . . exciting us to "give diligence to make our calling and election sure" and quicken our sluggish steps in the path of self-denying obedience.'

It is time that we turned to the psalm itself.

'Blessed are they whose ways are blameless,
   who walk according to the law of the Lord.
Blessed are they who keep his statutes
   and seek him with all their heart.
They do nothing wrong;
   they walk in his ways.
You have laid down precepts
   that are to be fully obeyed.
Oh, that my ways were steadfast
   in obeying your decrees!
Then I would not be put to shame
   when I consider all your commands.
I will praise you with an upright heart
   as I learn your righteous laws.
I will obey your decrees;
   do not utterly forsake me'

                             (Psalm 119:1-8).

1.
Walk this way

Psalm 119:1-8

'Blessed are they whose ways are blameless, who walk according to the law of the Lord' (v.1).

In his New Testament letter, James asks the question: 'Is anyone happy?' (James 5:13). What is the Bible's answer to the question: 'Who is the happy man?' What constitutes true Christian happiness? Is it having the broadest grin and the shiniest set of teeth, or the most exuberant personality and extrovert character?

A vital clue to the answer is that the word that the Bible uses for 'happy' (in both Old and New Testaments) is 'blessed'. 'Blessed' is a deep and rich word. It signifies the vast treasure of good things that the believer has both now (in possession) and yet to come (in prospect), all of which comes from God as the gift of His free grace. Toplady catches the spirit of this blessedness in his hymn which begins:

> How vast the benefits divine
> Which we in Christ possess!
> We are redeemed from sin and shame,
> And called to holiness,

and ends:

> Not one of all the chosen race
> But shall to heaven attain:
> Here they will share abounding grace,
> And there with Jesus reign.

The Lord Jesus Christ has much to say about this blessedness, this true happiness, and the character of those who possess it, in the opening verses of his Sermon on the Mount (Matthew 5:1-12).

It is surely significant that the 119th psalm begins with the word 'blessed', and since the psalm is all about God's Word it is not surprising that its definition of true blessedness is in connection with that Word. Or, as the psalmist himself puts it in the first verse, 'Blessed are they whose ways are blameless, who walk according to the law of the Lord.' So here is the answer to our question about true Christian happiness: it is the blessedness that comes only from walking in the way of God's Word.

Matthew Henry begins his commentary on this psalm with the statement: 'The psalmist here shows that godly people are happy people.' He adds, 'All men would be happy, but few take the right way; God has laid before us the right way, which we may be sure will end in happiness, though it be strait and narrow.' We would do well to recall that the Lord Jesus Christ Himself repulsed each of the devil's temptations in the wilderness with the response, 'It is written' — that is to say, 'Scripture says, God's Word declares . . .' Our prayer needs to be:

> Lord, be Thy Word my rule,
> In it may I rejoice;
> Thy glory be my aim,
> Thy holy will my choice.
>
> (Christopher Wordsworth).

All of this should impress upon us that the happy life is the obedient life — not going our own way and following our own fancies, but going God's way and following God's pleasure. And God's way and God's pleasure are set forth for us in His Word.

We may draw out from each of the first four verses of the psalm something further concerning this as it works out in practice. There are four things that we need.

1. A blameless walk

In the words of the old prayer, 'We have followed too much the devices and desires of our own hearts,' whereas God, our God, would have us 'walk according to the law of the Lord' (v.1). The only way to be blameless in the Christian life is to be hedged and hemmed in by God's Word — what a blessed restriction that should be! There is no blessedness in transgressing its borders, or branching out into avenues of adventure and investigation which His Word forbids. We must make God's Word, God's law, the rule of all our thoughts, all our actions and all our affections.

2. An undivided heart

The psalmist prays in another place, 'Give me, O Lord, an undivided heart.' This is another distinguishing mark of the happy, godly Christian. We long to be free from hyprocrisy and insincerity, unlike the worldling, whose heart is either not directed to God at all, or who seeks to 'get God's favour' while never actually submitting to God. True Christians desire to 'keep his statutes' and to 'seek him with all their heart' (v.2). Even the obedience, the keeping of God's statutes, is not for its own sake — nor, primarily, for the comfort it brings to the Christian, real though that is. Rather the aim is that God may be glorified in the undivided obedience of our hearts. Love to God Himself, first and foremost, is to be our spur and incentive.

> Blessed are the eyes that see Him,
> Blest the ears that hear His voice;
> Blessed are the souls that trust Him,
> And in Him alone rejoice;
>   His commandments
> Then become their happy choice.

(Joseph Swain).

3. An unsinning heart

Verse 3 looks like a very grand statement, as it says of believers, 'They do nothing wrong; they walk in his ways.' It seems to be speaking of perfection, and that is something we have not yet attained, nor ever shall until we are glorified. But what does the Lord Jesus Christ command? He says, 'Be perfect, therefore, as your heavenly Father is perfect' (Matthew 5:48). What does the Father Himself command? 'Be holy, because I am holy' (1 Peter 1:16). That is our goal, our desire: to be perfect, to be holy. Robert Murray M'Cheyne, in his famous hymn, 'When this passing world is done', looks forward to the time 'when I see Thee as Thou art, love Thee with unsinning heart'. Charles Wesley, in his equally famous 'Love divine, all loves excelling', cries out, 'Take away the love of sinning!' That, surely, is what the psalmist has in his mind. The thought of sinning — worse still, the love of sinning — should be increasingly horrifying to the happy, godly Christian. All that God tells us in His Word that He hates, we should hate, forsake and abhor; and, if we fall into it, we should lament bitterly. We must avoid sin carefully. We must wrestle energetically with temptation. We must deliberately flee from sin, and when we do sin (as, sad to say, we do and shall continue to do), how thankful we are for 1 John 2:1: 'If anybody does sin, we have one who speaks to the Father in our defence — Jesus Christ, the Righteous One'!

4. A firm recognition

God's precepts, which He has 'laid down', 'are to be fully obeyed' (v.4). That is why they have been given — not for consideration, not for examination, not so that we can express our opinions about them, but so that we should obey them.

> Trust and obey!
> For there's no other way
> To be happy in Jesus
> But to trust and obey.

> (J. H. Sammis).

So, not surprisingly, the psalmist turns to prayer to the Lord for help, for apart from Him we can do nothing. It is as if he acknowledges, 'Lord, I see what the happy life is; I desire with all my heart to live it; I hunger and thirst after it. But my problem is that again and again I cannot live it; I fail.' And he begins his prayer (v.5) with one of the most important words in the whole vocabulary of prayer — 'oh'. That little word signifies an intense sigh, an earnest desire, a heartfelt longing. Sometimes it is the only word we can utter. And by verse 8 he has worked through to the position of fresh resolve, but still in utter dependence upon the Lord: '*I will* obey your decrees; *do not* utterly forsake me.' In other words, 'Please do not leave me to my own strength, or my own heart, or my own resolutions.'

We need to see the clear connection and sequence here: the supreme authority of the Lawgiver, the total insufficiency of the creature, the full promise of the Saviour and the all-sufficiency of God's continuing grace.

Godly people are happy people. True Christian godliness and happiness are found in a sincere, consistent, practical, hearty, intelligent, earnest, active, stirring, humble, self-renouncing and self-distrustful delight in, and desire to keep, God's law, along with a ready confession that without divine grace we can do nothing at all. We are insufficient; he is all-sufficient!

'How can a young man keep his way pure?
   By living according to your word.
I seek you with all my heart;
   do not let me stray from your commands.
I have hidden your word in my heart
   that I might not sin against you.
Praise be to you, O Lord;
   teach me your decrees.
With my lips I recount
   all the laws that come from your mouth.
I rejoice in following your statutes
   as one rejoices in great riches.
I meditate on your precepts
   and consider your ways.
I delight in your decrees;
   I will not neglect your word'

(Ps. 119:9-16).

2.
Keeping pure

Psalm 119:9-16

'How can a young man keep his way pure? By living according to your word' (v.9).

Do you, as a Christian, continually cry from the heart: 'How can I keep my way pure? How can I steer a straight course, maintain a steady walk and be transformed into Christ's likeness with ever-increasing glory?' That is the question of the psalmist in this second section of the psalm, and while he couches the enquiry in terms of 'a young man' (rightly and suitably so, since youth is faced and fraught with peculiar temptations, difficulties and stumbling-blocks in the way of holiness), yet it is the question which should be the concern of every believer, whether young or old, whether we are thinking in terms of age or length of Christian experience.

1. A vital question

When Paul wrote to Timothy, 'Flee the evil desires of youth, and pursue righteousness, faith, love and peace, along with those who call on the Lord out of a pure heart' (2 Timothy 2:22), this was not only a word to young Timothy himself, but a vital exhortation for him to pass on to all those under his care, something which he was to make a regular part of his ministry.

The point is that our first need as sinners is to have our sins dealt with. Only God can forgive our sins. Only He can deliver us from the curse of sin, the dominion of sin and the misery of sin. We know how He has done that: through the blood of His one and only Son, the Lord Jesus Christ, shed on Calvary's cross for that very purpose. There is no other way for the sinner to be saved. No other person can save. No other religion can save. No other sacrifice can save.

> None other Lamb, none other name,
> None other hope in heaven or earth or sea,
> None other hiding-place from guilt and shame,
> None beside Thee!
>   (Christina G. Rossetti).

But although that is, unmistakably, our first need as sinners, it is not our only need. Nor does it exhaust the purpose for which Christ shed His blood and laid down His life for us. In Ephesians 1:4 Paul sets out the ultimate goal of our election and our salvation according to God's eternal plan and purpose: 'For he chose us in him [i.e, God chose us in Christ, the Father chose us in the Son] before the creation of the world to be holy and blameless in his sight.'

Hebrews 10:14 makes the very significant statement that the Lord Jesus Christ 'by one sacrifice . . . has made perfect [complete] for ever those who are being made holy'. There are two parallel lines of action in this passage. In Christ we have already been made complete; in Christ we are now being made holy. We see His accomplished, finished work at Calvary, as a result of which we have been made perfect or complete. He has done *all* for us. He 'has become for us wisdom from God — that is, our righteousness, holiness and redemption'; or again, 'You were washed, you were sanctified, you were justified in the name of the Lord Jesus Christ and by the Spirit of our God' (1 Corinthians 1:30; 6:11). Yet while *in principle* we have already been made perfect (for Christ is our holiness and sanctification just as much as He is our righteousness and redemption, and has done everything at Calvary to provide all that we shall ever need to all eternity), yet *in practice* the process of our sanctification, our being made holy as the people of God and being conformed into the image and likeness of Christ is going on all the time. We are (now, in the present) being made holy.

So the question, 'How can a young man keep his way

pure?' is one of the most important questions of all and a very real part of the Christian life.

2. A wise answer

What we may call 'a young man's question' is immediately followed by a wise man's answer: 'By living according to your word.' Only God's Word reveals clearly the true character of sin. Only God's Word urges upon us the absolute necessity of holiness. Only God's Word defines the nature of holiness and encourages us to holiness by its exceeding great and precious promises. Charles Bridges says, 'The value of the Word is inestimable as our means of walking with God in the hurry, business and temptation of the day.'

The psalmist shows us in this passage several different aspects of 'living according to [God's] word'. It is to be *wholehearted:* 'I seek you with all my heart' (v.10). It involves *worship:* 'Praise be to you, O Lord; teach me your decrees' (v.12). It is to be *joyful:* 'I rejoice in following your statutes as one rejoices in great riches' (v.14). It involves *meditation:* 'I meditate on your precepts' (v.15). And it is to be *careful:* 'I will not neglect your word' (v.16). But I want to concentrate particularly on the psalmist's testimony and attitude in verse 11: 'I have hidden your word in my heart.' To what end? 'That I might not sin against you.' Here we have, says C. H. Spurgeon, 'the best thing, in the best place, for the best of purposes'. But what does it mean to hide God's Word in our heart?

1. It means understanding it

This requires calling upon the Holy Spirit, whose special business and ministry it is to take God's Word, and all the precious things of Christ that are declared within it, and to make them clear, and asking that He would illumine and enlighten us. If we imagine that we can rely on our own understanding when it comes to hiding God's Word in our hearts we shall never make any progress at all! Spiritual things are spiritually discerned, that is, by the Holy Spirit teaching us.

And in the ordinary way that instruction must pass through *the mind* first in order for it to reach *the heart*.

2. It means believing it

One old preacher has put it this way: 'Until unbelief is broken down, the Word appeals for entrance in vain. When, however, it is welcomed by the hand of faith, it enters in and dwells there.' So long as any spirit of unbelief in the Word, or rebellion against it, remains in our hearts, the Word of God will not profit us or do us any good. We must welcome it into our hearts with true faith and humble submission: 'Humbly accept the word planted in you' (James 1:21).

3. It means loving it

Where there is no love for the Word, its effects and benefits are dulled considerably. If we love the Lord we shall love His Word and come to it with great delight. Later on the psalmist will exclaim, 'Oh, how I love your law!' (v.97). As an expression of that same testimony, Bishop Ryle commanded that his old Bible should lie on his heart in the grave.

4. It means memorizing it

The committing to memory of God's Word tends to be rather a lost art these days. One contributory factor may well be the increasing multiplicity and confusion of Bible versions that are used. Whatever the reasons for this neglect, there is great benefit in memorizing the Scriptures — not least as a means of assisting meditation on the Word. It is a work worth doing well, and can be made a most profitable part of family worship. Psalm 119 itself is a good place to begin! Philip Henry's daughter wrote in her diary on one occasion, 'I have of late taken some pains to learn by heart Psalm 119, and have made some progess therein.'

5. It means being directed by it

We remember the psalmist's declared purpose in hiding God's Word in his heart, which was that he should not sin against God. This reminds us of Christ's prayer for us in John 17:17: 'Sanctify them by the truth; your word is truth.' We need to understand, believe, love and memorize God's Word, but if all of that is to be fruitful it must issue in our being directed by the Word, framed by it, controlled by it, ruled by it, instructed by it, governed by it, kept on the right path by it, to the exclusion of all wrong paths. As we saw in the previous section, it was Scripture which the Saviour used in the wilderness in order to repel the temptations of the devil, and if we have truly hidden God's Word in our hearts in order to keep our way pure and so that we might not sin against God, then we shall follow Christ's example.

As a practical illustration of all this, let us pause to consider one or two examples of the wide-ranging application of this matter. It covers such things as the keeping of the Lord's Day (Exodus 20:8-11); quelling our rebellion against God's ways and dealings with us (Psalm 18:30); harbouring griefs and resentments against people (Matthew 6:14-15); the question of whom a believer is free, or not free, to marry (2 Corinthians 6:14-18); the directing aright of our thought lives (Philippians 4:8); right views of Christian fellowship (Hebrews 10:25) — and the list goes on and on!

We shall leave this section of the psalm with this comment from Matthew Henry: 'God's Word is a treasure worth laying up, and there is no laying it up safely but in our hearts. If we have it only in our houses and hands, enemies may take it from us. If only in our heads, our memories may fail us. But if our hearts are delivered into the mould of it, and the impressions of it remain in our souls, it is safe.'

'Do good to your servant, and I will live;
   I will obey your word.
Open my eyes that I may see
   wonderful things in your law.
I am a stranger on earth;
   do not hide your commands from me.
My soul is consumed with longing
   for your laws at all times.
You rebuke the arrogant, who are cursed
   and who stray from your commands
Remove from me scorn and contempt,
   for I keep your statutes.
Though rulers sit together and slander me,
   your servant will meditate on your decrees.
Your statutes are my delight;
   they are my counsellors'

(Psalm 119:17-24).

3.
Open my eyes!

Psalm 119:17-24

*'Open my eyes that I may see wonderful things in your
law' (v.18).*

When we were thinking about hiding God's Word in our
hearts, we saw that this involves, first of all, understanding
God's Word. We must understand it with our minds if we are
to hide it in our hearts. This matter of our understanding is
taken up now by the psalmist in this third section of the psalm.

We sometimes hear people ask the question: 'How can I
believe the Bible if I don't understand it?' For some this is a
genuine question; for others it can be a cloak for not wanting
to believe it. But whenever anyone cannot understand God's
Word, the fault is not in the Bible itself (i.e. that it needs to be
simpler, plainer, or whatever), but in us — in our darkened
minds and unbelieving hearts. Although it is not too familiar
a word these days, it is proper to speak in this connection of
the perspicuity of Scripture, which refers to its transparent
nature and clarity of expression. However, we need to have
our minds and our hearts opened to that transparency and
clarity; otherwise we shall not understand a word of it. This
'opening' is the Lord's own work; our spiritual eyes must be
opened for us, for we cannot perform this miraculous surgery
for ourselves. Only God can do it by His Holy Spirit. The
psalmist acknowledges this when he prays, 'Open my eyes
that I may see wonderful things in your law' (v.18).

This is a long process. In regeneration itself, when the Holy
Spirit causes us to be born again and makes us new creatures
in the Lord Jesus Christ, we are enabled to see all manner of
things in God's Word that we could never make anything of

before. As a result we come — with all our mind, heart, soul and strength — to love the Lord and to love His Word, believing it and embracing it.

But that is not the end of the matter. What I mean is this: do you understand *all* of the Bible? If someone were to turn, at random, to absolutely any text or portion, from Genesis through to Revelation, and ask you what it meant (not only on the surface, but in some of its unseen and hidden depths as well), could you tell him everything there was to know? I think not! I certainly know that I could not!

So what may we learn from verse 18? The teaching can be summarized under two simple headings.

1. There are wonderful things in God's Word

Our gracious God has already been pleased to show us so many of these by His Spirit. These are things that are hidden from multitudes — not only from the ignorant and unconcerned, but from the wise and learned, yet are revealed to little children. They are things that even angels long to look into; things that a man can receive only when they are given to him from heaven. 'The man without the Spirit does not accept the things that come from the Spirit of God, for they are foolishness to him, and he cannot understand them, because they are spiritually discerned' (1 Corinthians 2:14). What are these things, or some of them? We could sum them up as the wonders of God's creation, God's providence and God's grace.

Isaac Watts expresses it like this:

> The heavens declare Thy glory, Lord
> In every star Thy wisdom shines;
> But, when our eyes behold Thy Word,
> We read Thy name in fairer lines.
>
> The rolling sun, the changing light,
> And nights and days Thy power confess;
> But the blest volume Thou hast writ
> Reveals Thy justice and Thy grace.

And he concludes:

> Thy noblest wonders here we view,
> In souls renewed, in sins forgiven:
> Lord, cleanse my sins, my soul renew,
> And make Thy Word my guide to heaven.

Another hymnwriter, John H. Gurney, puts it this way:

> For all Thy gifts we bless Thee, Lord;
> But most for Thy redeeming blood,
> Thy pardoning grace, Thy quickening Word,
> These prompt our songs that God is good.

Where do we learn of God's glories of creation, providence and grace? In His Word! That is the place where He has chosen to reveal them and to set them before us. And the point is that it is owing to the precious and powerful ministry of the Holy Spirit that our eyes have been opened to see these wonderful things in God's Word. It is His doing, not ours, that the Bible is not a closed book to us, and so to Him alone belongs all the glory!

2. There are even more wonderful things in God's Word

These are things which the Holy Spirit of God has not yet declared or revealed to us. Do not misunderstand me. I most certainly do not mean that there are 'new revelations' for God to give us, or 'new words' for God to speak to us, as some urge in these days. God's Word, the Bible, is complete. Nothing is to be added to it; nothing is to be taken away from it. It stands as it is. What I do mean is that there are even more wonderful things in the inexhaustible treasures and ocean depths of God's Word that the Holy Spirit has not yet revealed to us. He has not yet been pleased to show them to us, though they are there all the time. I was struck with this comment from an old preacher: 'It is of great importance for us to be persuaded of this truth, that there are many things in the Bible still to be found out, and that, if we come in the right spirit, we may be made discoverers of some of them . . . However frequently we traverse the field, we shall perceive some fresh golden vein turning up its glance to us, and we shall wonder how our eyes were formerly holden that we did not see it. It was all there waiting for us, and we feel that more is waiting.' That is why, of course, humble, loving, earnest and dependent study and reading of God's Word, and regular attendance on the preaching of it, are so vitally important for all Christians and all churches.

'There are promises in God's Word that no one has ever yet found; there are treasures of gold and silver in God's Word that no one has yet taken pains to dig for; there are medicines in God's Word for the want of which many are poorly and dying.' Sometimes in our attitude to the Word of God we can be like someone who has for years and years been the owner of a magnificent country estate, without ever having realized exactly what was there.

All the way through our Christian life we need to have our eyes opened to behold fresh wonders from God's Word, as well as to be given a more spiritual, vigorous, felt and trans-forming perception of those wonders we have already beheld. The more our God teaches us by His Spirit, the readier we shall be to sit at His feet as those who feel they know nothing at all unless He teaches us. Our experience is rather like that of the man whose sight the Lord Jesus restored in Mark 8:22-26. In response to Jesus' question, 'Do you see anything?' he first replied, 'I see people; they look like trees walking around'; but soon afterwards it is recorded that 'Once more Jesus put his hands on the man's eyes. Then his eyes were opened, his sight was restored, and he saw everything clearly.'

The apostle Paul's prayer for the Ephesian Christians included this petition: 'I pray also that the eyes of your heart may be enlightened in order that you may know the hope to which he has called you, the riches of his glorious inheritance in the saints, and his incomparably great power for us who believe (Ephesians 1:18-19).

This is made all the more urgent in view of our status, which the psalmist describes in verse 19: 'I am a stranger on earth.' We are strangers and pilgrims here; we are not at home. Heaven is where we are going, and it is there that our Saviour, our kindred, our inheritance, our home and our hope are to be found. So if God were to hide His commands from us (v.19), where would we be?

Let us take to heart the message of Proverbs 6:21-23:

> 'Bind them upon your heart for ever;
>   fasten them around your neck.
> When you walk, they will guide you;
>   when you sleep, they will watch over you;
>   when you awake, they will speak to you.
> For these commands are a lamp,
>   and this teaching is a light,
> and the corrections of discipline
>   are the way to life.'

Commenting on this section of Psalm 119, Charles Bridges writes, 'Acquaintance with the Word of God supplies the place of friends and counsellors. It furnishes light, joy, strength, food, armour, and whatever [we] may need on [our] way homewards. In the light of this, is it any wonder that opened eyes (v.18) lead to longing souls?' (v.20).

Speaking of the psalmist, M'Cheyne writes, '[He] was not blind — his eye was not dim . . . and yet he felt that he needed more light. He felt that he needed to see deeper, to have the eyes of his understanding opened. He felt that if he had nothing but his own eyes and natural understanding he would not discover the wonders which he panted to see. He wanted divine teaching — the eye-salve of the Spirit; and therefore he would not open the Bible without this prayer.'

If the psalmist felt like that, then how much more should we?

'I am laid low in the dust;
    preserve my life according to your word.
I recounted my ways and you answered me;
    teach me your decrees,
Let me understand the teaching of your precepts;
    then I will meditate on your wonders.
My soul is weary with sorrow;
    strengthen me according to your word.
Keep me from deceitful ways;
    be gracious to me through your law.
I have chosen the way of truth;
    I have set my heart on your laws.
I hold fast to your statutes, O Lord;
    do not let me be put to shame.
I run in the path of your commands,
    for you have set my heart free'

(Psalm 119:25-32).

4.
Down but not out

Psalm 119:25-32

*'I am laid low in the dust; preserve my life according to
your word' (v.25).*

The Christian life is an amazing combination of ups and
downs. The moods of our lives as Christians can change so
rapidly — sometimes alarmingly so. And surely this is one of
the reasons why spiritual men and women of every age have
always loved the book of Psalms, for, however trite it might
seem to say it, all Christian life is there. We find the whole
range and span of Christian experience — from the rapturous
seasons, high up on the mountains, near to God and communing with Him, to the heavy seasons in the dark and deep val-
leys, when we cry out (if we have the strength), 'Where is the
blessedness we knew . . .?'

William Plumer wrote a massive commentary on the
Psalms and made this personal testimony in so doing: 'During
a Christian and ministerial life neither short, uneventful, nor
free from dark days and sharp sorrows [I have] never been
able to secure to [myself], or administer to others, full support
and abounding consolation, without a resort to the psalms.'

All of this introduces us to the fourth of the twenty-two
pearls on one string which comprise Psalm 119. In this section
verses 25 and 28 provide a sort of 'mirror image' of each
other, testifying to the reviving effects of God's Word — and
I use the phrase not to refer to revival in its classic sense (the
revival of religion and of the church) but rather to the renew-
ing and enlivening of the individual Christian from the
sloughs of despond and depression, from weariness of mind
and body and from sluggishness of soul.

1. The psalmist's condition

He says, 'I am laid low in the dust' ('my soul cleaveth to the dust', AV) and, 'My soul is weary with sorrow' ('my soul melteth for heaviness', AV).

In verse 25 the emphasis is upon his sense of spiritual dullness and deadness, and his utter powerlessness to do anything about it. The verb 'laid low' means 'loaded with weights'. In verse 28 the emphasis is on the psalmist's sense of being absolutely 'finished', as if to say, 'I'm through — it's all up with me.' The verb 'is weary' (AV, 'melteth') only appears twice elsewhere in the Old Testament — once in Job, where it is translated 'poured out' and once in Ecclesiastes, where it is rendered 'dropping through'. It evidently describes a fairly dire state, yet we must admit that it is one that is by no means unusual or exceptional in Christian experience. Maybe you can identify with the psalmist right now, even as you read this; or if not right now, maybe what he is saying 'rings bells' for you, as you think back and review your past experience.

If we ask, 'Why is he in this condition? What has brought it about? How did things ever get this bad?', here are a few of the reasons that have been suggested:

1. Depression or melancholy (troubles of mind, a heavy condition of heart and spirit).
2. An acute sense of his sinfulness, corruption and unworthiness before God, leading to an extreme sense of humiliation in His presence.
3. Afflictions that pressed heavily upon him.
4. Imminent peril of death.
5. Sickness of heart because of the earthboundness of his affections, and the impossibility he was finding of setting his mind and heart upon things above (the loss of spiritual realities so far as the felt sense and enjoyment of them was concerned).

At the end of the day there is no real need to choose between them. Maybe it was one or another of these things; probably it was a combination of some or all of them. Is that not often the case?

2. The psalmist's petition

He does not just sit there. Let's look again at the two key verses. In verse 25 he cries, 'Preserve my life' (AV, 'quicken me'); and in verse 28, 'Strengthen me.' Taken together these two expressions cover such ideas as to renew, strengthen, quicken, enliven, preserve alive, make to stand, establish and raise up. Plumer expounds the petition in this way: 'Revive my drooping graces, my drooping spirits and my failing health.' In other words, it represents a comprehensive calling upon God from a position of the psalmist's own utter helplessness and weakness, and of God's almighty power to revive and save.

He calls upon the name of the Lord his God; and so should we. 'The name of the Lord is a strong tower; the righteous run to it and are safe' (Proverbs 18:10).

3. The psalmist's plea

Here, however, is the nub of the matter, so far as the psalm's emphasis upon God's Word is concerned. In both verses 25 and 28 the psalmist enforces his petition to God with the phrase 'according to your word': 'Preserve my life according to your word.' 'Strengthen me according to your word.'

We see in these two verses that the way in which he expects God to answer his urgent petition and meet his extreme need is according to His Word. What does that mean? There is, surely, a double thrust: it means both in the ways set out in God's Word and also by means of that Word itself, as the psalmist meditates upon it and considers it, and as the Holy Spirit blesses it to his soul. And we should remember that, whether the psalmist was David or someone else, he had only a small portion of the Old Testament for this purpose, while we have all sixty-six books of the Bible!

In his delightful little book *From Grace to Glory*, Murdoch Campbell remarks that 'The law, or the Word of God, is not merely written in a book: it is also engraven on His people's heart.' He then goes on to give a list of what we may well describe as the reviving effects of God's Word: it is their guide through this dark world; it is their spiritual nourishment; it is their support in every trial; it is their source of joy and the substance of their song; it is, above all, the pure mirror in which they behold the glory of the Lord and whereby they are 'changed into the same image from glory to glory, even as by the Spirit of the Lord'; it is also the sword of the Spirit, by which they are to overcome all their enemies.

Another writer, commenting on the psalm, testifies that he has often needed the ministry of the reviving word for his own heart and has learned to find it in the daily reading of Scripture. He remarks, 'Let us seek to the Divine Physician amidst all feelings of failure, unworthiness and leanness of soul.'

In all this the psalmist is pleading with God to enable him, by means of the Word, to do all the duties, to resist all the temptations and to bear up under all the burdens which face him and press him day and night.

We should all, as believers, be found daily in regular, disciplined reading of the Word of God and meditation on it. By this means we shall be able continually to gather stores of material suitable for all the many situations we face in the course of our lives, both for our own benefit and for the help of our fellow believers. If we do not need all of it straight away, we can always put some of it by for a rainy day!

It is worth mentioning, before we leave this section, that one of the richest and most reviving themes of Scripture for the tossed and frail Christian is that of 'Christ in you, the hope of glory' (Colossians 1:27). Whatever their defects (for which age is without some?) our forefathers were, by and large, far more heavenly-minded than are the present generation of Christians. This was one of their great strengths and was put to blessed use when they were faced in their own hearts, in the church, or in the world around, with anything that might cause them to be downcast in their souls.

Paul Gerhardt wrote a lovely hymn which, in translation, goes like this:

'Midst the light, and peace, and glory
Of the Father's home,
Christ for me is waiting, watching,
Waiting till I come.

There, amidst the love and glory,
He is waiting yet;
On His hands a name is graven
He can ne'er forget.

There amidst the songs of heaven,
Sweeter to His ear
Is the footfall through the desert
Ever drawing near.

He and I, in that bright glory,
One deep joy shall share;
Mine, to be for ever with Him,
His, that I am there.

'Teach me, O Lord, to follow your decrees;
    then I will keep them to the end.
Give me understanding, and I will keep your law
    and obey it with all my heart.
Direct me in the path of your commands,
    for there I find delight.
Turn my heart towards your statutes
    and not towards selfish gain.
Turn my eyes away from worthless things;
    preserve my life according to your word.
Fulfil your promise to your servant,
    so that you may be feared.
Take away the disgrace I dread,
    for your laws are good.
How I long for your precepts!
    Preserve my life in your righteousness'
                                    (Psalm 119:33-40).

5.
Help!

Psalm 119:33-40

'Teach me, O Lord, to follow your decrees; then I will keep them to the end' (v.33).

An important and abiding lesson is emphasized here — that of our complete dependence upon God in the vital business of walking in His ways and living according to His Word. There is nothing that we can do without His divine help. We need Him continually. This is, of course, absolutely in line with the Saviour's great and trenchant statement: 'Apart from me you can do nothing' (John 15:5).

Taking our cue from the variety of verbs that are used in this section of the psalm, we can isolate three key strands of our dependence upon God and His Word.

1. Dependence on God for wisdom (vv. 33-34)

This comes through very clearly in the first two verses of this section, where the main verbs are 'teach me' (v.33) and 'give me understanding' (v.34). Sad to say, we need no teaching, encouragement or instruction in the way of sin. That is the way in which we would walk quite naturally, left to ourselves, without having to seek any advice or help for it. But to enter into the life of grace and faith (by way of regeneration and conversion), and to make continual and steady progress in that ongoing life of grace and faith as a believer, is a different matter altogether! Here we are in great need of continuing teaching, instruction and understanding.

In an earlier chapter we saw the crucial principle expressed in 1 Corinthians 2:14: 'The man without the Spirit does not accept the things that come from the Spirit of God, for they are foolishness to him, and he cannot understand them, because they are spiritually discerned.' Let us now put that passage alongside a verse from John's first letter: 'We know also that the Son of God has come and has given us understanding, so that we may know him who is true' (1 John 5:20). We cannot teach ourselves what we do not know (despite the well-known story of the man who, reporting on a Christian meeting he had attended somewhere, commented drily, 'None of us knew anything and we all taught each other.'). Moreover, spiritual knowledge and understanding are not things that we can stumble on by accident or through speculation; we can only receive them by divine revelation. As we commented in respect to verse 18, our eyes need to be opened if ever we are going to see wonderful things, or, indeed, anything, in God's Word. That is why our cry needs to be *continually*: 'Teach me, O Lord . . . Give me understanding.' Otherwise, however wise we may be in our own eyes, or we may appear to others, we shall remain in the dark.

Let us always remember the glorious promise of the Lord Jesus Christ regarding the ministry of the Holy Spirit: 'I have much more to say to you, more than you can now bear. But when he, the Spirit of truth, comes, he will guide you into all truth. He will not speak on his own; he will speak only what he hears, and he will tell you what is yet to come. He will bring glory to me by taking from what is mine and making it known to you. All that belongs to the Father is mine. That is why I said the Spirit will take from what is mine and make it known to you' (John 16:12-15).

There is a further point to observe here as well. Certainly, the psalmist acknowledges his complete dependence upon God for wisdom, teaching and understanding. But for what purpose? To what end? With what in view? So that he would be the cleverest theologian, the most famous preacher, or the one to whom everyone would look up and on whom they would bestow their praises? No trace of any such thing can be found at all. Notice carefully exactly what he says: 'Teach me, O Lord, *to follow your decrees*,' 'Give me understanding, *and I will keep your law*.' There are two more verbs there: 'follow' and 'keep'. They express the psalmist's desire to obey God, and that 'to the end' (i.e. throughout the whole of his life and course), and 'with all [his] heart' (for the way the heart goes, the whole man goes).

Matthew Henry comments that the psalmist desires to be taught, not the notions or language of God's Word, but the way of it — the way of applying it to himself, the way of being governed by it, the way of knowing always what God would have him do.

Let this be an encouragement to us, then, that we may, and indeed should, ask boldly for 'light from above', and that it will be given freely to us and will always be found to be amply sufficient. If God Himself, by His Spirit, is our Teacher, then we need not (nor shall we be able to) plead ignorance as our excuse for disobedience to His Word.

2. Dependence on God for direction (vv. 35-37)

What a practical psalm this is! Moving on to verses 35-37, we start once again by noticing how the verbs express dependence upon God: 'direct me' (v.35), 'turn my heart' (v.36), 'turn my eyes' (v.37). Just as there can be no following God's decrees or understanding God's law without divine enlightenment, so there can be no diligent pursuit of God's way, nor any undivided commitment to the things of God, without His divine energy being given to our wills (so that they may be obedient) and His divine ardour settled in our hearts (so that we may truly love His laws).

The verb 'direct' (AV, 'make me to go') is well chosen to express our need and dependence, and the verb 'turn' (AV, 'incline', connected first with 'my heart' and then with 'my eyes'), reminds us how easily we 'do our own thing'. As the old prayer puts it so well, 'We have erred and strayed from Thy ways like lost sheep. We have followed too much the devices and desires of our own hearts.'

In this cry for direction the psalmist desires, quite specifically, not to be turned 'towards selfish gain', but to be turned 'away from worthless things'. When John Bunyan's pilgrims were obliged to pass through Vanity Fair, beset on every side with all sorts of temptations and allurements, they stopped up their eyes and ears and quickened their pace — a striking

reproof to us, who so often loiter and gaze and covet those
things to which, as Christians, we should be dead. In this connection, Matthew Henry observes that the psalmist prays for
restraining grace, that he might be prevented and kept back
from that which would hinder him in the way of his duty; and
for *constraining* grace, that he might not only be kept from
everything that would obstruct his progress heavenward, but
that he might have the grace that was necessary to forward
him in that progress.

3. Dependence on God for renewal (vv. 37-40)

As we have already found, themes which have already been
considered arise again at various points in the psalm, but
never in the manner of vain repetition or unnecessary dupli-
cation. The psalmist is never just filling up the space!

The key verb this time, in verses 37-40, is 'preserve' or
'renew' (AV, 'quicken'). It occurs twice (vv.37,40) and ties in
with what we saw in the previous section on the reviving
effects of God's Word to quicken our needy souls. Once
again, it is practical results that are in view as the goal of this
preservation or renewal: the fear of God (v.38), and God's
righteousness (v.40).

The first of these, 'Preserve my life according to your
word . . . so that you may be feared,' includes the sense of
such preservation as a safeguard from sin. In this, we are
reminded of Joseph, Genesis 39, who, when under pressure
in the face of the seductive designs of Potiphar's wife, uttered
the cry, 'How then could I do such a wicked thing and sin
against God?' The comment has been made that the fear of
God evidences itself in dread of His displeasure, desire of His
favour, regard for His excellencies, submission to His will,
gratitude for His benefits and conscientious obedience to His
commands. Oh, for such fear of God in our daily life and
walk, for which we are cast upon Him in filial dependence!
We may add that there is also in the psalmist's statement here
the expression of his renewed confidence and trust in God
and his devotedness to His work, redeeming the time and
improving all his opportunities.

The second petition, 'Preserve my life in your righteousness,' gathers together (as I understand it) two vital things: the plea, 'Oh, for a livelier view and grasp of your own spotless righteousness, you who are my God!' and the cry, 'Oh, for a more vigorous exercise of righteousness and grace in my own life, walk and character as a child of God!' Perhaps such a cry reaches its all-time high point in David's words in Psalm 17:15:

> 'And I — in righteousness I shall see your face;
> when I awake, I shall be satisfied with seeing your
> likeness.'

'May your unfailing love come to me, O Lord,
    your salvation according to your promise;
then I will answer the one who taunts me,
    for I trust in your word.
Do not snatch the word of truth from my mouth,
    for I have put my hope in your laws.
I will always obey your law,
    for ever and ever.
I will walk about in freedom,
    for I have sought out your precepts.
I will speak of your statutes before kings
    and will not be put to shame,
for I delight in your commands
    because I love them.
I lift up my hands to your commands, which I love,
    and I meditate on your decrees'

(Psalm 119:41-48).

6.
At liberty

Psalm 119:41-48

*'I will walk about in freedom, for I have sought out
your precepts'* (v.45).

The Christian's liberty or freedom in walking according to
God's Word is a most delightful and evocative theme, and is
the one which occupies the psalmist's attention in this next
section of Psalm 119. The centrepiece is verse 45 and the
psalmist's happy testimony there to walking about in freedom
(AV, 'at liberty'). There are three profitable ways of
approaching the subject.

1. Our natural condition was one of bondage

That is something we can never recall too often. John Bunyan
gave to what we might call his spiritual autobiography the
magnificent and highly appropriate title, *Grace Abounding to
the Chief of Sinners.* In it he writes that 'It is profitable for
Christians to be often calling to mind the very beginning of
grace.' When we do that, we cannot help but recall that our
natural condition as sinners was one of the most grievous bondage, before we knew anything of God's grace towards us in
the Lord Jesus Christ, before our minds and hearts were
moved by anything of the love of Christ or the pull of God's
Spirit and before our consciences were convicted with a
proper sense of our sin and guilt.

This is the backdrop from the past to the psalmist's statement in verse 45 about his life and walk in the present. Now
he walks about in freedom (and he will continue to do so).

But it was not always so. Remember Charles Wesley's testimony:

> Long my imprisoned spirit lay
> Fast bound in sin and nature's night.

What sort of bondage were we in?

We were in bondage to sin

The Lord Jesus Christ says, 'I tell you the truth, everyone who sins is a slave to sin' (John 8:34). And we all sinned! The unbeliever is under the rule and dominion of sin, sold to sin, under the thumb of sin, in sin's grip. Such language is by no means too extravagant, even though so many in these days (preachers included) would seek to water down talk of sin and the sinfulness of sin. Yet (and here is sin's own deceitfulness!) it is what the old writers used to call a 'senseless' slavery, which means one that you do not realize or admit that you are in. You think you are 'your own man', free to live as you please. It is a bondage from which the sinner has no power to deliver himself, for we were 'dead in sin'; and what can a corpse do to give itself life?

We were in bondage to Satan

The Bible makes clear that Satan is the ruler of the kingdom of sin and darkness. He is the devil, the ancient serpent, the one who is a liar and the father of lies. Samuel Bolton likens him to a jailer, 'who holds poor souls down as under brazen bars and behind iron gates not to be broken'. He adds, 'If a man is in bondage it is some relief to him to have a merciful jailer. But this adds to the misery of the sinner that he has a cruel jailer.' He also says, 'Satan is a cruel tyrant, who rules in the hearts of the children of disobedience.'

We were in bondage to God's law

That is to say, we were under its curse, for 'All who rely on observing the law are under a curse, for it is written: "Cursed is everyone who does not continue to do everything written in the Book of the Law'" (Galatians 3:10). That was us!

All of this describes how we once were, what our natural state and condition used to be. We continued in that sad and sorry plight until the glorious Lord Jesus Christ came and set us free. To use Bunyan's imagery again (this time from *The Holy War*), our city of Mansoul was in the grip of the evil Diabolus, who used every ruse, intrigue and force to keep us under his sway and spell, until that happy day when Prince Emmanuel secured the victory over him and set us free to be His own!

2. Our new condition is one of freedom

We have been called 'out of darkness into [God's] wonderful light' (1 Peter 2:9). The Saviour has said, 'If the Son sets you free, you will be free indeed' (John 8:36). Sin is slavery. Divine grace, lavished upon us in the Lord Jesus Christ, God's own and only Son, has brought us out of the prison-house, unlocked our chains and fetters, and set us at large.

The word 'freedom' in verse 45 is translated in another place in this same psalm as 'broad' or 'boundless', and the sense is that of walking at large, walking free, rather than being hemmed in or blocked up. Charles Wesley again:

> Thine eye diffused a quickening ray,
> I woke, the dungeon flamed with light;
> My chains fell off, my heart was free;
> I rose, went forth, and followed Thee.

Wonderful salvation — again, we cannot recall it too often! And our freedom, corresponding point by point to our bondage, is freedom from sin, from Satan and from God's law.

Freedom from sin

We have been given freedom from the penalty of sin (death and hell), from its guilt and its dominion, and (increasingly, and one day, completely!) from its presence and its power. How? Because 'God made him who had no sin to be sin for us, so that in him we might become the righteousness of God' (2

Corinthians 5:21). In other words, because of the gospel, the good news of the great exchange; Christ has become our Saviour and substitute, dying for the sins of the elect people of God, on the cross at Calvary. And in and through, and on account of, Him we have been made righteous and given righteousness — the righteousness of God.

Freedom from Satan

Our old master has been overpowered and evicted, and we now serve a new Master, the Lord Jesus Christ. The strong man has been dealt with by the one who is stronger than he is (compare Luke 11:21-22).

Freedom from God's law

By that is meant not the anti-nomianism that some (evangelicals included) teach, namely that the law of God has no place in the believer's life, that it is null and void, so to speak; but rather that we have been given freedom, or been set free, from the curse of the law, on the gospel grounds of Galatians 3:13: 'Christ redeemed us from the curse of the law by becoming a curse for us, for it is written: "Cursed is everyone who is hung on a tree."'

We are walking in the King's highway. We are God's 'freedmen'. We are journeying, as Spurgeon puts it, 'from the Egypt of bondage to the Canaan of rest'.

3. Our normal condition should be one of obedience

By normal, I mean in this context, regular, consistent, stable.

There is a beautiful paradox in the psalmist's words when he says, 'I will walk about in freedom.' When you are really bound, you think you are free. Yet to be really free is to be bound — not to sin, but to Christ, to be a blessed bond-slave of the Lord Jesus, whose service (unlike any other) is perfect freedom. This paradox is expressed in these lines:

> Make me a captive, Lord,
> And then I shall be free . . .

Imprison me within Thine arms
And strong shall be my hand.

(George Matheson).

James describes God's Word as 'the perfect law that gives freedom' (James 1:25), and so it is. We may be sure of this: God's Word defines true Christian liberty and freedom for us, its genuine nature, bounds and limits. We are free only when we move within that sphere. If we step outside it and rebel against God's Word and take issue with His law, that is not an exercise of Christian liberty! Any desire to cast off the restraints of God's Word points back in the old direction of bondage, not in the new direction of freedom. Every Christian only walks in true liberty and freedom when (in the language of verse 45) he seeks out God's precepts. In his classic work, *The True Bounds of Christian Freedom*, Samuel Bolton comments that while the law drives us to the gospel to be saved, the gospel directs us back to the law in order to frame our way of life. And that very way of life, walking at liberty according to God's precepts, is defined further as trusting in God (v.42), putting our hope in God's laws (v.43), always obeying God's law (v.44), testifying to God's statutes without shame (v.46), delighting in God's commandments (v.47) and reaching out our hands for God's commandments (v.48 — the phrase means an eager desire to grasp and enjoy them).

Charles Bridges remarks, 'Every sin is a fresh chain of bondage under the check of a cruel master . . . every fresh chain by which we bind ourselves to the Lord, makes us more free.' We must never abuse our Christian liberty or allow it as a licence for sin. Rather we must maintain it, enjoy it and glorify Christ in it, and we are to encourage fellow believers and challenge the world by showing what a delight obedience to Christ and the service of Christ really is!

The apostle Paul writes, 'It is for freedom that Christ has set us free. Stand firm, then, and do not let yourselves be burdened again by a yoke of slavery' (Galatians 5:1). Isaac Watts chimes in:

Make me to walk in Thy commands,
'Tis a delightful road;
Nor let my head or heart or hands
Offend against my God.

'Remember your word to your servant,
   for you have given me hope.
My comfort in my suffering is this:
   Your promise preserves my life.
The arrogant mock me without restraint,
   but I do not turn from your law.
I remember your ancient laws, O Lord,
   and I find comfort in them.
Indignation grips me because of the wicked,
   who have forsaken your law.
Your decrees are the theme of my song
   wherever I lodge.
In the night I remember your name, O Lord,
   and I will keep your law.
This has been my practice:
   I obey your precepts'

(Psalm 119:49-56).

7.
People of the book

Psalm 119:49-56

*'Your decrees are the theme of my song wherever
I lodge'* (v.54).

We are familiar with the phrase 'going by the book'. How true
that is — or should be — for Christians! We are to be people
of *the* book, and that book, of course, is the Bible. This is the
keynote of this seventh section of the psalm, focusing upon
verse 54. We love, we read and we recommend books about
the Bible ('books about the Book'), and that's fine, but above
all we need to be people of the book itself.

Spurgeon has a famous remark about Bunyan, to the effect
that it does not matter where you prick him, his blood is bibline! In other words, he has the Bible flowing through his
veins! He is saturated in Scripture. Well, that is equally true
of our psalmist. He testifies, 'Your decrees are the theme of
my song wherever I lodge.' For the NIV's 'wherever I lodge',
the AV has 'in the house of my pilgrimage', which calls to
mind the testimony of godly Jacob as an old man in Genesis
47:9: 'The years of my pilgrimage are a hundred and thirty.
My years have been few and difficult, and they do not equal
the years of the pilgrimage of my fathers.'

1. The Christian is a pilgrim

The author of Psalm 119, (whether David or not) speaks of his
life in terms of this sort — 'wherever I lodge', 'the house of my
pilgrimage'. In that he is a 'type' of all those who are, by
grace, children of the living God. And if it was David who

wrote this psalm, it shows that even his palace in Jerusalem was no more permanent in his view, nor more important to him, than a lodging-place!

A pilgrim is a person who is travelling through one country on his way to another. There is an old song which captures a biblical truth: 'This world is not my home, I'm just a-passing through.' You can express this in different ways, and the Bible does exactly this, using words like 'aliens', 'foreigners' and 'strangers in the world'. Here we have no abiding, no enduring, no continuing city. Here we have no permanent resting-place for the soles of our feet, no true home, but we 'nightly pitch our moving tent a day's march nearer home', and one day we will strike our tents for the very last time on earth and be ushered and welcomed into eternal heavenly habitations. Here we have (in earthly terms) no lasting goods or possessions. Here we are for ever longing for, and looking towards, our heavenly dwelling, 'the city with foundations, whose architect and builder is God' (Hebrews 11:10); 'an inheritance that can never perish, spoil or fade — kept in heaven' (1 Peter 1:4); the many mansions of the Father's house.

We are not ashamed of this. Far from it, we glory in it! But (let it be said to our shame) we do not rejoice in it, glory in it and long for it to anything like the degree to which our forefathers did. Present-day evangelicalism, contemporary preaching and average Christian experience are most appallingly earthbound and know all too little, if anything, of the spirit expressed so vitally and so beautifully by the Puritan preacher John Preston who, at his death, could say, 'I shall change my place but not my company.'

2. The Christian is a singing pilgrim

The psalmist says here that God's decrees are the theme of his song. Pilgrims often sing as they make their journey. It helps to combat weariness, it reminds them that they belong together and it helps to cover the miles of the journey. Interestingly, straight after Psalm 119 comes that section of the psalter from Psalms 120-134, the fifteen songs of ascents.

More likely than not, these psalms were sung by the Jewish
pilgrims coming from the north, south, east and west at festi-
val time and making their way up to Jerusalem.

So the Christian is a singing pilgrim on the journey to
heavenly Jerusalem, heavenly Zion. Many Christian hymns
take up this fruitful and expressive theme.

> Children of the heavenly King,
> As ye journey, sweetly sing;
> Sing your Saviour's worthy praise,
> Glorious in His works and ways.
>
> We are travelling home to God
> In the way the fathers trod;
> They are happy now, and we
> Soon their happiness shall see.
>
> Shout, ye little flock and blest!
> You on Jesus' throne shall rest;
> There your seat is now prepared,
> There your kingdom and reward.
>
> Lift your eyes, ye sons of light;
> Zion's city is in sight;
> There our endless home shall be,
> There our Lord we soon shall see.
>
> Fear not, brethren; joyful stand
> On the borders of your land;
> Jesus Christ, your Father's Son,
> Bids you undismayed go on.
>
> Lord, obediently we go,
> Gladly leaving all below:
> Only Thou our Leader be,
> And we still will follow Thee.

To that fine hymn from John Cennick could be added Isaac
Watts' 'Come, we that love the Lord', and many another.
Here is just a taste from Watts:

> Then let our songs abound,
> And every tear be dry;
> We're marching through Immanuel's ground
> To fairer worlds on high.

David's testimony in Psalm 40:3 concerning the Lord is that 'He put a new song in my mouth, a hymn of praise to our God.' We have cause to sing because we know the salvation of the Lord, the joy and peace of the Lord and the forgiveness and blessing of the Lord. We are able to sing because, while we have our trials (not only the trials which are common to all men, but the many trials which are peculiar to Christians as well), we also have our matchless joys and encouragements, which the unbeliever knows nothing whatsoever about! Even when we are 'worst off' or in our 'poorest way', we are in a far, far happier condition than the unbeliever when he is at his best. Godly poverty is better than unhallowed riches. The believer's sickness is preferable to the worldling's health. Our abasement is more welcome than the sinner's honours. It is good to remind ourselves from time to time of 2 Corinthians 4:7-12, and of Elihu, in the book of Job, who spoke of God giving His people 'songs in the night' (Job 35:10).

Delitzsch comments that God's decrees are the believer's songs, 'which give him spiritual refreshing, sweeten the hardships of the pilgrimage, and measure and hasten his steps'. Worth recording at this point also is a threefold division of this 54th verse of the psalm by William Jay under the title 'The Cheerful Pilgrim'. His points are these:

1. A good man views his residence in this world as only the house of his pilgrimage.
2. The situation, however disadvantageous, admits of cheerfulness.
3. The sources of his joy are derived from the Scriptures.

3. The Christian has the best songbook

That, indeed, is what Jay has implied in the analysis just quoted. What is it — precisely — that forms the theme of the psalmist's song? 'Your decrees', he says. Why and how, though, is God's Word so wonderful, precious and suitable a songbook for the believer in his pilgrimage — so much so that he would not exchange it for a whole library of other books?

Firstly, it reveals clearly the end of our journey.

Secondly, it contains all the directives we need as to how to travel so as to reach our journey's end.

Thirdly, it contains the history of our fellow-pilgrims who have travelled this way before us and have now arrived at the heavenly goal.

Fourthly, it runs over with all the *promises* of God to support us along the way; all the *prescriptions* of God to heal us from the diseases we meet along the way (such as suffering from loss of first love to Christ, spiritual depression, perplexity over God's will, backsliding, and so on); all the *precepts* of God to guide us along the way; and all the *provisions* of God to nourish and encourage us along the way. In a word, as Paul wrote to Timothy in a celebrated passage, 'You have known the holy Scriptures, which are able to make you wise for salvation through faith in Christ Jesus. All Scripture is God-breathed and is useful for teaching, rebuking, correcting and training in righteousness, so that the man of God may be thoroughly equipped for every good work' (2 Timothy 3:15-17).

> There is a book that comes to me,
> From One who spake of old,
> Who calls with shepherd-voice the flock
> That wanders from the fold.
>
> There is a book whose pages white
> A wondrous love reveal —
> A love once wounded unto death,
> The wounds of sin to heal.
>
> There is a book whose promises
> I all my life may plead;
> They shine like stars above the night
> Of my exceeding need.

There is a book whose pilgrim songs
Are sweet as songs of spring:
I hope to sing them till the day
When I shall see the King.

(F. A. Jackson).

We have the God of the book. We have the book of our God. We are the people of God. Let us also be the people of the book!

'You are my portion, O Lord;
   I have promised to obey your words.
I have sought your face with all my heart;
   be gracious to me according to your promise.
I have considered my ways
   and have turned my steps to your statutes.
I will hasten and not delay
   to obey your commands.
Though the wicked bind me with ropes,
   I will not forget your law.
At midnight I rise to give you thanks
   for your righteous laws.
I am a friend to all who fear you,
   to all who follow your precepts.
The earth is filled with your love, O Lord;
   teach me your decrees'

                                   (Psalm 119:57-64).

8.
My portion

Psalm 119:57-64

'You are my portion, O Lord; I have promised to obey your words' (v.57).

How do you think of God? As your Father, your Redeemer, your refuge . . .? Do you ever think of Him as your portion? Is that a characteristic of God that means anything special to you? It certainly meant a lot to the psalmist; and the more we consider it, the richer a description of God it presents itself to be. There are several different aspects of God as the believer's portion which are worth considering, and I shall mention four of them.

1. Personal possession

For a start, this very title for the Lord reminds us that He is personally possessed by the believer. Personal possession, of course, is the very language of the covenant of grace, for God says to us, 'I will be *your God* and you will be *My people.*' This very language and thought is to the fore in what the psalmist says in verse 57: '*You* are *my* portion, O Lord.'

What is a 'portion'? The Hebrew word has the basic idea of 'dividing' and recalls the ancient custom among the Jews of dividing family inheritances so that each person had his allotted portion. This comes through, you remember, in Jesus' famous parable of the lost (or prodigal) son in Luke 15. The AV of Luke 15:12 reads, 'Give me the portion of goods that falleth to me' (NIV, 'Give me my share of the estate'), as a result of which request the father divided his property between his two sons. Just from that one illustration we can see the progression and association of ideas — dividing, inheritance, possession (in the sense of what belongs to someone and cannot be taken away from him).

The Bible applies this to God and His people, to God and the believer. Putting it personally, God, having set His love upon me in Christ before the foundation of the world and having saved me by His free and sovereign grace, has become my inheritance, my part, my lot, my possession — my portion. This is expressed most beautifully in two classic Old Testament texts which are worth quoting in full:

> 'Whom have I in heaven but you?
>   And earth has nothing I desire besides you.
> My flesh and my heart may fail,
>   but God is the strength of my heart
>   and my portion for ever'
>
> (Psalm 73:25-26).

> 'Because of the Lord's great love we are not consumed,
>   for his compassions never fail.
> They are new every morning;
>   great is your faithfulness.
> I say to myself, "The Lord is my portion;
>   therefore I will wait for him"'
>
> (Lamentations 3:22-24).

What is actually comprised in God being my portion? In a word — everything! It includes His great salvation, His everlasting love, His continual presence, His infallible guidance, His unfolding purposes, His mysterious providences, His unerring wisdom, His fatherly care, His never-failing promises, His heavenly rest — and that only begins the list! It all adds up to a lavish statement and a glorious assurance of the complete sufficiency of God to all those whom He has made His own.

Thomas Brooks puts it like this: 'A man that has God for his portion is the rarest and happiest man in the world; he is like the morning star in the midst of the clouds; he is like the moon when it is at full; he is like the flower of the roses in the spring of the year; he is like the lilies by the springs of waters;

he is like the branches of frankincense in the time of summer; he is like a vessel of gold that is set about with all manner of precious stones.' Believer, who has God as your portion, do you recognize that as a description of yourself?

But while we feast upon the blessedness of this, let us be sure that we do not miss the challenge. Those who testify, 'You are my portion, O Lord,' do not just say it in words. They demonstrate it in their lives: 'I have promised to obey your words.' Otherwise theirs is at best a dubious, and at worst a false testimony.

2. Hearty seeking

The second thing worth noticing is that, as their portion, the Lord God is heartily sought by His people. David said on one occasion,

> 'O God, you are my God,
>   earnestly I seek you;
> my soul thirsts for you,
>   my body longs for you,
> in a dry and weary land
>   where there is no water'

>   (Psalm 63:1).

On another occasion he said,

> 'Hear my voice when I call, O Lord;
>   be merciful to me and answer me.
> My heart says of you, "Seek his face!"
>   Your face, Lord, I will seek'

>   (Psalm 27:7-8).

Since he knew the incomparable blessing of having God for his portion, the psalmist's continual concern was to grow and advance into a deeper, fuller knowledge of God and experience of God. Hence he said, 'I have sought your face with all my heart; be gracious to me according to your promise' (v.58). And he knew where God, whom he sought and desired, was to be found — in His Word; 'your promise' (v.58); 'your statutes' (v.59); 'your commands'. (v.60).

That most spiritual of letter-writers, Samuel Rutherford, writing to one of his regular correspondents, Lady Kenmure, a godly and noble woman, spoke of drawing near to God in this way: 'To the end you may get thus earnest, it were good to come often into terms of speech with God, both in prayer and hearing of the Word. For this is the house of wine where you meet with your Well-Beloved. Here it is where He kisses you with the kisses of His mouth and where you feel the smell of His garments . . . You must wait upon Him and be often communing with Him.'

To the same end, the hymn-writer penned these lines:

> More about Jesus in His Word,
> Holding communion with my Lord;
> Hearing His voice in every line.
> Making each faithful saying mine.
>
> (Eliza E. Hewitt).

3. Comfort in experience

There is more: as His people's portion, the Lord is comfortingly felt. There is nothing distant, nothing remote or second-hand about this relationship. In the face of the malice of his enemies, the loneliness of his position and the mocking of his testimony (v.51), and at that hour of the night when so often everything seems hardest, blackest, loneliest and most hopeless and desolate (v.62), he comforted his soul in, and directed his devotions to, the One who is his portion:

> 'Though the wicked bind me with ropes,
>   I will not forget your law.
> At midnight I rise to give you thanks
>   for your righteous laws.'

4. Corporate enjoyment

To this we may add a fourth note — namely, that as their portion the Lord is corporately enjoyed by His people. This is what the psalmist tells us in verse 63 when he says, 'I am a friend to all who fear you, to all who follow your precepts.' He associates himself quite deliberately and firmly with all such people. He has in mind, surely, the fellowship of kindred minds, the communion of saints — the situation pictured in Malachi 3:16, where 'Those who feared the Lord talked with each other.' On our way to church, after the service, when we visit Christian friends, what and whom do we talk about? Do we enjoy our God and portion together? Do we speak of His grace? Do we study His Word? Do we consider His ways? Do we approach His throne together?

To sum up the teaching of this section of the psalm, here is another marvellous paragraph from Thomas Brooks: 'Luther counsels every Christian to answer all temptations with this short saying, "I am a Christian"; and I would counsel every Christian to answer all temptations with this short saying, "The Lord is my portion." O Christian, when Satan or the world shall tempt thee with honours, answer, "The Lord is my portion"; when they shall tempt thee with riches, answer, "The Lord is my portion" . . . and when this persecuting world shall tempt thee with the loss of thy estate, answer, "The Lord is my portion"; and when they shall threaten thee with the loss of thy liberty, answer, "The Lord is my portion"; and . . . with the loss of friends . . . and . . . with the loss of life, answer, "The Lord is my portion."'

We conclude with Toplady's incomparable testimony to what it is to have God — the God of the Word — as our portion:

A Sovereign Protector I have,
Unseen, yet for ever at hand,
Unchangeably faithful to save,
Almighty to rule and command.
He smiles, and my comforts abound;
His grace as the dew shall descend;
And walls of salvation surround
The soul he delights to defend.

Inspirer and Hearer of prayer,
Thou Shepherd and Guardian of Thine,
My all to Thy covenant care
I sleeping and waking resign.
If Thou art my Shield and my Sun,
The night is no darkness to me;
And fast as my moments roll on,
They bring me but nearer to Thee.

Kind Author, and ground of my hope,
Thee, Thee, for my God I avow;
My glad Ebenezer set up,
And own Thou hast helped me till now.
I muse on the years that are past,
Wherein my defence Thou hast proved;
Nor wilt Thou relinquish at last
A sinner so signally loved!

'Do good to your servant
   according to your word, O Lord.
Teach me knowledge and good judgement,
   for I believe in your commands.
Before I was afflicted I went astray,
   but now I obey your word.
You are good, and what you do is good;
   teach me your decrees.
Though the arrogant have smeared me with lies,
   I keep your precepts with all my heart.
Their hearts are callous and unfeeling,
   but I delight in your law.
It was good for me to be afflicted
   so that I might learn your decrees.
The law from your mouth is more precious to me
   than thousands of pieces of silver and gold'
                                    (Psalm 119:65-72).

9.
Hard times

Psalm 119:65-72

'Before I was afflicted I went astray, but now I obey your word.'
'It was good for me to be afflicted so that I might learn your
decrees' (vv.67,71).

Did you know that Martin Luther once said, 'I never knew the
meaning of God's Word, until I came into affliction. I have
always found it to be one of my best schoolmasters'? That is
no superficial, or super-sanctified, statement. Rather it
acknowledges from Christian experience the vital link established in these verses of the psalm between God's Word and
the blessings of affliction. The sanctifying purposes and blessings of affliction are many and varied — such as, a greater
dependence upon God, the building of spiritual character,
the forming of greater likeness to Christ, the development of
a more tender conscience and the opportunity for more sensi-
tive ministry to others along the lines of 2 Corinthians 1:3-7.

In this ninth section of the psalm, the psalmist's angle is
both very important and very interesting. He ties the whole
business of the purpose of God in afflicting His children to a
greater, deeper, more wholehearted knowledge of, and
obedience to, God's Word. The key verses are 67 and 71,
which may be set out like this:

1. Before affliction: I went astray.
2. As a result of affliction: I obey your word.
3. Affliction was good for me.
4. Why? It taught me your Word.

The fact is that all too easily we do not see it this way at all,
but it is high time that we did! Can we each of us draw this contrast between before and after affliction, which is so real and

genuine for the psalmist? Can we acknowledge with respect
to those afflictions, trials and disappointments which God has
been pleased to order for us personally, that they were good
for us? Can we now say as a result of them, that we prize,
know, understand, relish and obey the Word of God all the
more, since affliction expounded and explained it to us?

1. Two illustrations

Let me use a couple of illustrations, one on the sea and the
other on the land.

Supposing a terrible storm drove a ship, on which you were
a passenger, into harbour for refuge when still some way from
your destination. Would that be a good thing? On the surface,
no! You would be more likely to regard it as frustrating,
delaying and costly. But suppose that during this enforced
time in port, a serious flaw was found in one of the ship's
engines, which would have put it in immense danger if it had
remained at sea, or that it was discovered that the vessel had
sprung a leak and was taking in so much water that to have
sailed on would have been absolutely calamitous. What then?
Would the delay have been a good thing? Yes indeed! So it is
in the Christian life, as God fulfils all of His good, wise and
gracious purposes for us. Sometimes He tosses us around in a
sea of affliction in order to drive us into the harbour of His
Word, so that there — while we are laid aside for a season and
cast upon Him in a special way — His Word, in the power of
His Spirit, may press upon our consciences, exposing our sins
and showing us our weaknesses and making such things as
God's covenant, God's grace, God's attributes, God's promises, God's providences and God's mercies become wonder-
fully precious, powerful and personal to us in a fresh way.

To take another example, supposing you were out on a
long walk (a real map, compass and walking boots job!) and
that, whether from negligence, over-confidence, or whatever, you failed to consult the map, ignored all the signposts
and got completely off the track, but still blindly and foolishly
pushed on, until a mishap finally forced you to stop. Would
that be a good thing? On the surface, by no means! But if the
mishap brought you to your senses, if it made you examine

your map again and start using your compass properly, and if it had the effect of making you take proper notice of all the signposts and warnings of dangers — what then? Wouldn't it prove a good thing? Surely it would! In the same way, we all know those times in our lives when the Bible becomes dry as dust and we leave it unread, when our appetite for spiritual things loses its keenness and its edge, when we begin to hanker after this and that, and to neglect the clear signposts God has given us in His Word as to how to live the Christian life, and we begin to pay the price. Then God steps in with a trial, an affliction, or an obstacle that He puts in our path, or he lays a restraining hand on our shoulders to keep us from wandering any further down sinful and foolish paths. He shows us again, from His Word, the glory of His salvation and the wonder of His love. He reminds us again, from His Word of all our mighty privileges as children of God and our responsibility to live in Him and to Him. He convinces us again, from His Word, of all our utter dependence upon Him in every way and shows us that without Him we were helplessly lost.

2. The results of affliction

What is the result of all this? The result is that we can at last testify with the psalmist, 'Before I was afflicted I went astray, but now I obey your word,' and 'It was good for me to be afflicted so that I might learn your decrees.'

God's book sets out for us the way to heaven: but not only how to begin on that way, but how to continue on it as well. In heaven itself, not least, we shall have ample cause to say to God and to one another, 'It was good for me to be afflicted.' Such affliction, remarks Charles Bridges, marks Christ's wisdom no less than His love. 'This', he says, 'is the gracious rod by which He scourges back His prodigal children to Himself — this is the wise discipline by which He preserves them from the poisoned sweetness of carnal allurements and keeps their hearts in a simple direction towards Himself, as the well-spring of their everlasting joy.'

Isn't this the very testimony of Scripture itself? The well-known teaching of Hebrews 12 is on just this point:

'And you have forgotten that word of encouragement
   that addresses you as sons:

"My son, do not make light of the Lord's discipline,
   and do not lose heart when he rebukes you,
because the Lord disciplines those he loves,
   and he punishes everyone he accepts as a son."'

'Endure hardship as discipline; God is treating you as sons.
For what son is not disciplined by his father? If you are not
disciplined (and everyone undergoes discipline), then you are
illegitimate children and not true sons. Moreover, we have all
had human fathers who disciplined us and we respected them
for it. How much more should we submit to the Father of our
spirits and live! Our fathers disciplined us for a little while as
they thought best; but God disciplines us for our good, that
we may share in his holiness. No discipline seems pleasant at
the time, but painful. Later on, however, it produces a har-
vest of righteousness and peace for those who have been
trained by it. Therefore, strengthen your feeble arms and
weak knees! "Make level paths for your feet," so that the
lame may not be disabled, but rather healed' (Hebrews 12:5-
13).

Let us close this section with two passages drawn from personal experience of this truth. The first is another snippet
from a letter from Samuel Rutherford to Lady Kenmure, and
it is followed by John Newton's classic hymn-testimony.

'The thorn is one of the most cursed, angry and crabbed
weeds that the earth yields — and yet out of it springs the
rose, one of the sweetest-smelling flowers and most delightful
to the eye that the earth has. Your Lord shall make joy and
gladness out of your affliction, for all His roses have a sweet
smell. Wait for the time when His holy hand shall hold them
to your nose.'

I asked the Lord that I might grow
   In faith, and love, and every grace,
Might more of His salvation know,
   And seek more earnestly His face.

'Twas He who taught me thus to pray,
  And He, I trust, has answered prayer;
But it has been in such a way
  As almost drove me to despair.

I hoped that in some favoured hour
  At once He'd answer my request;
And, by His love's constraining power,
  Subdue my sins, and give me rest.

Instead of this, He made me feel
  The hidden evils of my heart,
And let the angry powers of hell
  Assault my soul in every part.

Yea, more, with His own hand He seemed
  Intent to aggravate my woe,
Crossed all the fair designs I schemed,
  Blasted my gourds, and laid me low.

'Lord, why is this?' I trembling cried,
  'Wilt Thou pursue Thy worm to death?'
''Tis in this way,' the Lord replied,
  'I answer prayer for grace and faith.

'These inward trials I employ,
  From self and pride to set thee free,
And break thy schemes of earthly joy,
  That thou mayest seek thy all in Me.'

                              (John Newton).

'Your hands made me and formed me;
   give me understanding to learn your commands.
May those who fear you rejoice when they see me,
   for I have put my hope in your word.
I know, O Lord, that your laws are righteous,
   and in faithfulness you have afflicted me.
May your unfailing love be my comfort,
   according to your promise to your servant.
Let your compassion come to me that I may live,
   for your law is my delight.
May the arrogant be put to shame for wronging me
     without cause;
   but I will meditate on your precepts.
May those who fear you turn to me,
   those who understand your statutes.
May my heart be blameless towards your decrees,
   that I may not be put to shame'

(Psalm 119:73-80).

10.
Well stirred

Psalm 119:73-80

'May those who fear you rejoice when they see me' (v.74).

'May your unfailing love be my comfort' (v.76).

'May my heart be blameless towards your decrees' (v.80).

One thing has been clear from the start: the psalmist medi-tates often upon God's Word. Remember what he said in verse 15: 'I meditate on your precepts and consider your ways.' The more we meditate on God's Word, the more profitable and enjoyable an exercise we find it to be. Reading brings a truth into our heads, while meditation brings it into our hearts. Thomas Watson has remarked: 'The reason we come away so cold from reading the Word is because we do not warm ourselves at the fire of meditation.'

However, the writer of Psalm 119 did not fail to warm him-self at the fire of meditation (even though he possessed only a fraction of the complete Bible that you and I have). As a result, his times spent with God in His Word were continually profitable. The section of the psalm now before us — the tenth — shows us one particular benefit: the Word of God stirring up urgent prayer. What a fuel to prayer the reading, meditation and preaching of God's Word should be! Our experience ought to be (much, much more than it is) that we have no option but to turn from the Word directly to pray.

We can isolate four strands or directions of the psalmist's praying here, as God's Word stirred him in his soul.

1. Prayer for understanding

The psalmist has been impressed (even overwhelmed and overawed) by learning of God that 'Your hands made me and formed me.' God is his Maker, the God of his being, his very life. As for himself, he is God's workmanship. But, wonderful as all of that is, there is something even more wonderful. He belongs doubly to God: not only by creation, but by re-creation; not only by birth, but by rebirth. And so he pleads for understanding to learn more of God's commands, more of His Word, more of His truth, more of His ways and more of His power — in a word, more of God Himself, in order to serve God, glorify God and enjoy Him all the more. So he prays, 'Give me understanding to learn your commands' (v.73).

This is very much the prayer of a spiritual man; it is not the prayer of the natural man. It is significant that the more people have been taken in with the theory of evolution, the less (inevitably) have they had any sense of indebtedness to God as the fountain and giver of life, and the less have they had any desire to understand, learn or obey God's commands. They have become, in very truth, godless.

If we would be spiritual people, the psalmist here should be a model for us to imitate. The more God shows us of Himself from His Word, the more we realize that there is of Him to know. And the more we realize that there is of Him to know, the less we feel that we already know of Him so far. And the less we feel that we already know of Him so far, the more we are stirred up in prayer before Him: 'Lord, show me, give me, illumine me, unlock for me more of Yourself.'

Every Christian should have an insatiable appetite for God, and never be able to get enough of Him and His Word. Is that a good description of you?

2. Prayer for fellowship

How cheering it is for one child of God to have fellowship with another! That is one reason (though only one) for the exhortation in Hebrews 10:25: 'Let us not give up meeting together, as some are in the habit of doing, but let us encourage one another — and all the more as you see the Day approaching.' We are not to live as freelancers or lone rangers. The psalmist testifies here of himself: 'I have put my hope in your word' (v.74), and so desired greatly the fellowship of like minds and hearts: 'May those who fear you rejoice when they see me' (v.74). 'May those who fear you turn to me, those who understand your statutes' (v.79). This is in strong and obvious distinction to the others described in verse 78: 'May the arrogant be put to shame for wronging me without cause.'

'As the believer finds trouble from the world, he prays that he might find help from the Lord's people. The very sight of our Father's family is cheering . . . it is painful therefore to see Christians often walking aloof from each other and suffering coldness, distance . . . and distrust to divide them from their brethren.' So writes Charles Bridges. It is sobering and shattering to discover that it is to Christians that Paul writes when he says, 'If you keep on biting and devouring each other, watch out or you will be destroyed by each other' (Galatians 5:15).

There are various choice Bible phrases that come to mind: 'All the believers were one in heart and mind' (Acts 4:32). 'You are the body of Christ, and each one of you is a part of it' (1 Corinthians 12:27). 'We can comfort those in any trouble with the comfort we ourselves have received from God' (2 Corinthians 1:4). 'Carry each other's burdens, and in this way you will fulfil the law of Christ' (Galatians 6:2). 'Those who feared the Lord talked with each other' (Malachi 3:16). 'Let the peace of Christ rule in your hearts, since as members of one body you were called to peace. And be thankful. Let the word of Christ dwell in you richly as you teach and admonish one another with all wisdom, and as you sing psalms, hymns and spiritual songs with gratitude in your hearts to God' (Colossians 3:15-16). Perhaps this would be a good moment to read through Psalm 133!

Give us the Lord's people every time! Behind this, of course, lie the glories of sovereign grace, the wonders of electing love, the sweetness of pardoning mercy and the certainties of particular redemption — for these are the causes of our belonging to God and to one another! I was struck by this remark from Alec Motyer: 'If you have a proper fear of God

in your heart you will have a proper reverence for the people
of God in your life.'

3. Prayer for maturity

I use the word 'maturity' deliberately. We know from the previous section of the psalm that the psalmist had been suffering
great affliction of some sort. Maybe it was linked with the
people he mentions in verse 78, the arrogant who had been
wronging him without cause. He has already acknowledged,
'It was good for me to be afflicted so that I might learn your
decrees' (v.71), but he is not satisfied with himself. He still
desires to grow more in grace as a result of affliction. He still
desires, with an earnest spiritual desire, to enjoy God, to be
drawn into closer communion with Him and to explore more
of the immensities of God. Hence the references to God's
faithfulness, His unfailing love and His compassion:

> 'I know, O Lord, that your laws are righteous,
>   and in faithfulness you have afflicted me.
> May your unfailing love be my comfort,
>   according to your promise to your servant.
> Let your compassion come to me that I may live,
>   for your law is my delight'
>
> (vv.75-77).

Once more it is a question of 'appetite'! The psalmist craves
for more of an experimental knowledge of God. Let us not
lose that good old word, 'experimental'; it means practical, or
based on experience. He desires more submissive acceptance
and trust, more holy and godly 'resignation' and contentment
with all of God's ways.

4. Prayer for blamelessness

'May my heart be blameless towards your decrees, that I may
not be put to shame,' prays the psalmist (v.80). The word
translated 'blameless' has the sense of 'sound', but not mere
soundness of doctrine for its own sake (cold orthodoxy);

rather, it means heart-soundness, soundness of life and walk. There is, of course, absolutely no substitute for sound, biblical doctrine. That is clear enough from this 119th Psalm, but the psalm also impresses upon us repeatedly the importance of the doctrine being fruitful in the life: there must be truth *and* godliness, belief *and* piety.

Right at the beginning of the psalm we were challenged with the blessedness of those 'whose ways are blameless, who walk according to the law of the Lord' (v.1), and the importance of keeping our way pure 'by living according to your word' (v.9). The Word and purity; the Word leading to purity — we can never consider this matter too much. Even though absolute blamelessness, purity and holiness will be ours only in glory, yet they are still to be before us continually as our great aim and goal. So Paul urges, 'Aim for perfection' (2 Corinthians 13:11). Let us meditate carefully upon Christ's command in Matthew 5:48: 'Be perfect, therefore, as your heavenly Father is perfect,' and the classic thrust of 1 Peter 1:16: 'It is written: "Be holy, because I am holy."' Then we should bring in Hebrews 12:14, with its reminder that 'Without holiness no one will see the Lord.' We must blame ourselves for every shortfall and refuse to excuse ourselves over any sin — always!

We should also notice the second part of verse 80. The dreaded consequence of hypocrisy in this matter is being put to shame — by God and before God.

May the Word which stirred the psalmist to prayer stir us also. You know how it is sometimes, I am sure. We come to prayer (whether secret prayer or the prayer meeting) and all seems cold and lifeless. Then how often have we turned to the Word — and oh, the themes that have been suggested! Out flow our confession, praise, adoration, thanksgiving, supplication and worship! May it ever be so — God's Word stirring up His people to pray!

'My soul faints with longing for your salvation,
    but I have put my hope in your word.
My eyes fail, looking for your promise;
    I say, "When will you comfort me?"
Though I am like a wineskin in the smoke,
    I do not forget your decrees.
How long must your servant wait?
    When will you punish my persecutors?
The arrogant dig pitfalls for me,
    contrary to your law.
All your commands are trustworthy;
    help me, for men persecute me without cause.
They almost wiped me from the earth,
    but I have not forsaken your precepts.
Preserve my life according to your love,
    and I will obey the statutes of your mouth'
(Psalm 119:81-88).

11.
Divine comfort

Psalm 119:81-88

'My eyes fail, looking for your promise; I say, "When will you comfort me?"' (v.82).

It is always lovely and heart-warming to see how one Scripture dovetails with another. You can see it in, for example, the way in which the book of Leviticus in the Old Testament and the letter to the Hebrews in the New Testament are so very much a pair. But you can often see it on a smaller scale, as in this new section of the psalm. These verses dovetail with Romans 15:4 and the apostle Paul's remark there concerning 'the encouragement [AV, 'comfort'] of the Scriptures'. Here is the complete verse: 'For everything that was written in the past was written to teach us, so that through endurance and the encouragement of the Scriptures we might have hope.' And in the very next verse of that chapter, the apostle goes on to call God 'the God who gives endurance and encouragement'. So the mutual theme both of the psalmist and the apostle is clear: the comfort, encouragement, endurance and hope which the believer derives from God directly through His Word.

The psalmist is cast down for two reasons, it seems. One is his own mortal frailty, and the other is unjust persecution. He says, 'My soul faints with longing for your salvation . . . my eyes fail, looking for your promise . . . I am like a wineskin in the smoke.' This last reference is no doubt to a leather bottle of kid or goat skin found in humble dwellings. People would keep many articles (dry and liquid) in such bottles, which, for security, were suspended from the roof or hung against the walls. They would soon become black with smoke and gather minute particles of soot, for in the peasant dwellings where they were most commonly found there were seldom any chimneys. So whenever a fire was kindled, the smoke could only escape through an opening in the roof or by the door. When the bottles contained solids rather than liquids they became shrunk, contracted and shrivelled up, and this is exactly how the psalmist feels because of trouble and affliction, trial and persecution.

Matthew Henry (who takes the psalmist to be David) observes: 'David was thus wasted by age, sickness and sorrow. See how affliction will mortify the strongest and stoutest of men! David had been of a ruddy countenance, as fresh as a rose; but now he is withered, his colour is gone, his cheeks are furrowed.'

Yet in the midst of his weakness and of persecution, which cause him to cry, 'When will you comfort me?' (v.82) and 'How long must your servant wait?' (v.84), in his very deep need of solid and enduring comfort, where do his heart and mind incline? See what he says:

'I have put my hope in your word' (v.81).
'I do not forget your decrees' (v.83).
'All your commands are trustworthy' (v.86).
'I have not forsaken your precepts' (v.87).
'I will obey the statutes of your mouth' (v.88).

So then, here once again in our study of Psalm 119 we are presented with a very practical question: how does God's Word become to us such a major source of encouragement, comfort and hope? It is worth searching out some of the answers. Let me suggest seven lines of thought for our spiritual meditation.

1. It sets and keeps God Himself before us

At the heart of the Word of God is the covenant of God; and at the heart of God's covenant is His gracious covenant promise: 'I will be their God, and they will be my people' (Jeremiah 31:33). There is not the slightest doubt that one of the most fundamental lacks from which we suffer as the people of God (amazing as it may seem) is lack of the knowledge of God. We seem to know so little about Him, and to apply so little even of what we do know to our daily life and experience. How vital, therefore, that we should be found much in the Word, deriving comfort and encouragement from the covenant God who is the God of comfort and encouragement! He is the all-wise God. He knows the end from the beginning. He works everything according to the counsel of His will, as the One seated upon the throne of the universe. He is 'God Most High . . . who fulfils his purpose for me' (Psalm 57:2). 'We know that in all things God works for the good of those who love Him, who have been called according to His purpose' (Romans 8:28). He 'has blessed us in the heavenly realms with every spiritual blessing in Christ' (Ephesians 1:3). 'In his great mercy he has given us new birth into a living hope through the resurrection of Jesus Christ from the dead' (1 Peter 1:3). We have the blessed assurance that He will meet all our needs 'according to his glorious riches in Christ Jesus' (Philippians 4:19). What a wonderful God and Father He is to us!

2. It bids us not to fear

It does so, of course, on the solid basis of what we have just observed concerning God Himself. It is a case of 'Since this God is our God, therefore we need not fear'! Or, in the actual language of Scripture, 'What, then, shall we say in response to this? If God is for us, who can be against us?' — and so, you remember, the apostle continues in that magnificent final portion of Romans 8!

Spurgeon makes a lovely comment on this point: '"Fear not" is a plant which grows very plentifully in God's garden. If you look through the lily beds of Scripture you will continually find by the side of other flowers the sweet "Fear nots" peering out from among doctrines and precepts, even as violets look up from their hiding-places of green leaves.' A little later he adds, 'Now I gather from the plentifulness of 'Fear nots', even in the Old Testament, that the Lord does not wish His people to be afraid, that He is glad to see His people full of courage, and especially that He does not love them to be afraid of Him. He would have His children treat Him with confidence.'

3. It commands us to find all our joys in Him

Isn't this the very spirit of the psalmist throughout this 119th Psalm? We see it also in that classic testimony from Psalm 73 where Asaph testifies,

> 'Whom have I in heaven but you?
>   And earth has nothing I desire besides you.
> My flesh and my heart may fail,
>   but God is the strength of my heart
>   and my portion for ever.'

Dr Edward Payson made the following admission: 'Christians might avoid much trouble if they would believe that God is able to make them happy without anything else. God has been depriving me of one blessing after another; but as every one was removed, He has come in and filled up its place; and now, when I am a cripple, and not able to move, I am happier than ever I was in my life before, or ever expected to be. If I had believed this twenty years ago, I might have been spared much anxiety.'

4. It pictures for us the saints who have gone on before us

It depicts for us the saints of God who have travelled to Zion before us, those who have discovered, by grace, that the chief end of man is indeed to glorify God and to enjoy Him for ever. We see Enoch, walking with God in a hostile environment; Abraham, finding God his shield and exceeding great reward; Job, submitting to all the mysterious providences in the permissive will of God, and saying, at the end of it,

> 'My ears had heard of you,
>   but now my eyes have seen you.
> Therefore I despise myself
>   and repent in dust and ashes'

> (Job 42:5-6).

We see David, strengthening himself in God; Daniel, being protected in the lion's den by the One who shut the lion's mouths; and his three friends in the burning fiery furnace, accompanied by one who looked 'like a son of the gods'. We see Paul, who in 2 Corinthians 11 gives the catalogue of his sufferings, yet can say in the next chapter, 'When I am weak, then I am strong.'

5. It gives us many great and precious promises

A. W. Pink says of the divine promises that they 'make known the good pleasure of God's will to His people, to bestow upon them the riches of His grace. They are the outward testimonies of His heart, who from all eternity loves them and foreappointed all things for them and concerning them.' How many of them can you bring immediately to memory and write down?

6. It urges us to fix our hearts and minds on things above

In other words, it sets before us again and again the practical duty and importance of spiritual-mindedness and heavenly-mindedness, which is to have heaven in us long before we are actually in heaven. It is impossible to measure the unspeakable comfort that such an attitude will give, or the comfort that we deny ourselves, or of which we rob ourselves (to God's own dishonour) if we neglect this duty.

7. It directs us to the felt ministry of the Comforter

The Holy Spirit, in all the blessed variety of His divine ministry, is the Comforter, the Paraclete, which means the One who is called alongside to help. Where would we be without Him?

'Your word, O Lord, is eternal;
   it stands firm in the heavens.
Your faithfulness continues through all generations;
   you established the earth, and it endures.
Your laws endure to this day,
   for all things serve you.
If your law had not been my delight,
   I would have perished in my affliction.
I will never forget your precepts,
   for by them you have preserved my life.
Save me, for I am yours;
   I have sought out your precepts.
The wicked are waiting to destroy me,
   but I will ponder your statutes.
To all perfection I see a limit;
   but your commands are boundless'

(Psalm 119:89-96).

12.
For ever and ever

Psalm 119:89-96

> *'Your word, O Lord, is eternal; it stands firm in the heavens' (v.89).*

For ever settled in the heavens,
Thy Word, O Lord, shall firmly stand;
Thy faithfulness shall never fail;
The earth abides at Thy command.

Thy Word and works unmoved remain,
Thine every purpose to fulfil;
All things are Thine and Thee obey,
And all as servants wait Thy will.

I should have perished in my woe
Had I not loved Thy law divine;
That law I never can forget;
O save me, Lord, for I am Thine.

The wicked would destroy my soul,
But in Thy truth is refuge sure;
Exceeding broad is Thy command,
And in perfection shall endure.

That metrical version of this twelfth section of Psalm 119 highlights the grand doctrine of these eight verses. The first of them (v.89) says it all: God's Word is firm, fixed, sure, certain and settled. The same note is also struck in verse 91: 'Your laws endure to this day.'

There are two striking New Testament counterparts to this vital theme and facet of God's Word:

> 'Heaven and earth will pass away, but my words will never pass away'
>
> (Matthew 24:35).

> '"All men are like grass,
>   and all their glory is like the flowers of the field;
> the grass withers and the flowers fall,
>   but the word of the Lord stands for ever"'
>
> (1 Peter 1:24-5).

One of Job's so-called 'comforters' said that 'Man is born to trouble as surely as the sparks fly upward' (Job 5:7). Indeed Job himself said at one point, 'Man born of woman is of few days and full of trouble' (Job 14:1). How often we feel it to be so! Our faith is often weak, our love is often low and our joy tends to ebb and flow like an incoming and outgoing tide. Our circumstances can sometimes seem more changeable than there are days in the week. We face illness, poverty, disappointment, bereavement, unemployment, persecution and all manner of trying things. As the hymn-writer puts it in those famous lines, '. . . helpers fail and comforts flee'.

Lest such considerations should overwhelm us (as sometimes they almost do) we need the cordial and perspective of this new section of the psalm, with its leading theme of the firmness and stability of God's Word. Why is God's Word firm? Because God Himself, whose Word it is, is eternal, firm, unchangeable and sure. His Word resembles Himself. God is in heaven, not upon earth. He is not in any way subject to the changeableness and restlessness which seem to characterize the earth; and God's Word, like God Himself, 'stands firm in the heavens' (AV, 'is settled in heaven'), and that eternally (AV, 'for ever').

There are many lessons we can draw from this theme which will bring us great blessing as we meditate on it and apply it to our lives. In this chapter we shall pursue three avenues of thought, each of which should inspire the believer with ample grounds for praise and prayer.

1. God's designs and purposes are firm

This is true in respect of both his grace and his providence, both of which are revealed most fully in Scripture. The firmness of God's purposes of *grace* (or, we might say, God's gracious purposes) is seen in His sovereign decree of election. God says, 'I will have mercy on whom I have mercy, and I will have compassion on whom I have compassion' (Romans 9:15). This is well expressed in question 20 of the Westminster Shorter Catechism and its answer:

'*Question*: Did God leave all mankind to perish in the estate of sin and misery?

'*Answer*: God having, out of His mere good pleasure, from all eternity, elected [chosen] some to everlasting life, did enter into a covenant of grace, to deliver them out of the estate of sin and misery, and to bring them into an estate of salvation by a Redeemer.'

The book of Revelation describes the elect people of God in most beautiful terms: 'a great multitude that no one could count, from every nation, tribe, people and language, standing before the throne and in front of the Lamb' (Revelation 7:9).

The firmness of God's *providence* is equally sure. He knows what He is doing now, why He did what He did in the past and what He still intends to do. He knows what He ordains and what He permits. We are bidden by the Lord Jesus Christ to pray, 'Your will be done.' The truth is, of course, that His will *must* be done, for says the Lord,

'I am God, and there is no other.
I am God, and there is none like me.
I make known the end from the beginning,
    from ancient times, what is still to come.
I say: My purpose will stand,
    and I will do all that I please.
From the east I summon a bird of prey;
    from a far-off land, a man to fulfil my purpose.
What I have said, that will I bring about;
    what I have planned, that will I do'

(Isaiah 46:10-11).

We sometimes make a plan which seems a good one, but later we find flaws in it, or it becomes too expensive or difficult, or proves unworkable, or we find we have taken on too much, and so we have to abandon it. It is not so with God! Whether on a global, international, national or personal scale (right down to what happens in my little life), God is in complete control.

In the final sermon in his magnificent book, *Christian Experience*, Donald MacDonald makes an important observation regarding grace and providence. This is what he says: 'For the sake of convenience we usually distinguish between the realm of grace and the realm of providence, but they are actually the same. They are not two distinct realms, for there is no dividing line between the grace of God and the providence of God. He works in them equally and is the sole worker of them.'

2. God's covenant and promises are firm

These, too, are settled in heaven. God will never turn aside from His eternal covenant — that covenant sealed with the blood of the mediator and surety shed at Calvary. Has He not promised His people that He will be our God for ever and ever?

> 'Has he not made with me an everlasting covenant,
> arranged and secured in every part?'
>
> (2 Samuel 23:5).

> 'May the God of peace, who through the blood of the eternal covenant brought back from the dead our Lord Jesus . . .'
>
> (Hebrews 13:20).

Right here in our psalm, the psalmist testifies, 'Your faithfulness continues through all generations' (v.90). This is *seen in creation*: 'You established the earth, and it endures' (v.90). What does the earth rest on? Nothing! It 'floats' in space; but when I say it 'floats', I do not mean that it drifts around or hurtles about all over the place; it keeps to its orbit. It endures in the place where God has put it and keeps it.

What is seen in creation is also *known by experience*. This comes through in verses 92-93, where, surely, the psalmist has in mind God's application to him in a personal way of all the covenant promises, such as, 'Never will I leave you, never will I forsake you'; 'I will be a Father to you'; 'The eternal God is your refuge, and underneath are the everlasting arms', and many others, all indicating that the Lord is fighting for, nourishing, protecting, loving, honouring, vindicating, guiding and rescuing His people. Many a time we have passed through deep waters, but have we ever yet drowned?

3. God's gospel and his power to bless it are firm

'Your laws endure to this day, for all things serve you' (v.91). The power of the gospel is clearly stated in Romans 1:16: 'I am not ashamed of the gospel, because it is the power of God for the salvation of everyone who believes.' Other passages which demonstrate this clearly are John 6:37; John 5:24; Acts 2:21 and Mark 16:16.

God will not reverse or recall what has gone forth from His lips. So we preach and testify and witness, and we plead with God to bless His own Word that goes out. And we believe Him when He promises in these generous divine terms:

> 'As the rain and the snow
>   come down from heaven,
> and do not return to it
>   without watering the earth
> and making it bud and flourish,
>   so that it yields seed for the sower and bread for the
>   eater,
> so is my word that goes out from my mouth:
>   It will not return to me empty,
> but will accomplish what I desire
>   and achieve the purpose for which I sent it'
>   (Isaiah 55:10-11).

This is heaven's gospel, preached from heaven's book, in the power of heaven's Spirit!

> Dear dying Lamb! Thy precious blood
> Shall never lose its power,
> Till all the ransomed church of God
> Be saved, to sin no more.
>
> (William Cowper).

How are we to put the lessons of this section into practice?

1. We have to learn to trust God at all times, however much or however long the fulfilment of His Word might seem to be delayed.

2. We have to learn to trust God as the one sure and safe anchorage for our souls, amidst all the changes round about us, and all the vanities of the world which seek to entice us away from Him.

3. We must learn to trust God as He is here revealed to be — faithful and true in Himself, and faithful and true to His Word and His gospel. We must never lean on the fancies and impressions of our own often feeble, fickle and faithless hearts, but only on Him. He is altogether and eternally trustworthy.

'Oh, how I love your law!
   I meditate on it all day long.
Your commands make me wiser than my enemies,
   for they are ever with me.
I have more insight than all my teachers,
   for I meditate on your statutes.
I have more understanding than the elders,
   for I obey your precepts.
I have kept my feet from every evil path
   so that I might obey your word,
I have not departed from your laws,
   for you yourself have taught me.
How sweet are your words to my taste,
   sweeter than honey to my mouth!
I gain understanding from your precepts:
   therefore I hate every wrong path'

                      (Psalm 119:97-104).

13.
In love

Psalm 119:97-104

'Oh, how I love your law! I meditate on it all day long' (v.97).

Can you honestly say that you love God's Word? The psalmist could, and did; and so should every believer. Loving God's Word flows directly from loving God. So, loving God's Word should be one of the marks of every true believer and every true church.

In writing this section I was struck by something Spurgeon has included in his *Treasury of David* from among the various materials he gathered. It is a description of the 'recognizable marks' of a vehement love for God's Word. He lists eight of them and I record them here for our consideration.

1. Profound reverence for the authority of the Word.
2. Admiration for its holiness.
3. Jealousy for its honour. God's servant feels acute pain when men slight it in any way.
4. Respect for its wholeness. The psalmist would not divorce precepts from promises, nor ignore a single statement in it.
5. Indefatigability, or unweariedness, in its study.
6. Eager desire to obey it.
7. Forwardness in praising it.
8. Activity in spreading it abroad.

I am sure you will agree that that is a most valuable list — and one, moreover, which may act as a helpful assistant in our examination of our own hearts to see whether we really do love God's Word or not.

Let me put this question, and then seek to begin to answer it: 'Why should we love God's Word?' Why should the psalmist's clear and unashamed testimony in verse 97 be our own?

1. Because it is God's Word

The emphasis is on 'God's': it is *God's* Word. If we look through this thirteenth section of the psalm we notice straight away that the psalmist uses the personal pronoun 'your', referring to God, in every verse: 'your law' (v.97); 'your commands' (v.98); 'your statutes' (v.99); 'your precepts' (v.100); 'your word' (v.101); 'your laws' (v.102); 'your words' (v.103); 'your precepts' (v.104). How is that for making his point?

Have you ever been accused of 'bibliolatry'? It means 'worshipping the Bible'. There are far worse things we could be called! But, in fact, the accusation is unjust, for only God Himself is to be worshipped — not His creation, His book or anything else that He has made, done or given; so we are not called to be 'Bible worshippers'. But we are — most certainly and happily — to be identified and distinguished as Bible-believers (believing every word of it!) and Bible-lovers.

There are plenty of people who may read the Bible, be fascinated or intrigued by it, have respect for it, and even study or preach it. But only the born-again believer, the sinner saved by grace, loves the Bible. We love it because we have been brought, through divine grace, in the power of the Spirit of God, to know and love the Author of the Bible. We love it because it is His. As one preacher says, 'It is our Father's legacy, the commandment and promises of Him who sticketh closer than a brother. It is the counsel and loving assurance of our best and truest Friend.' Amen to that! Our God breathed out His Word (2 Timothy 3:16). He wrote it; He has given it to us; it testifies chiefly of Him, and we see Him there in a rich display of His glory. It would make no sense at all to say, 'I love the Lord,' and not be able to go on to say, 'I love your Word.'

In his hymn 'The Lord Jehovah reigns', Isaac Watts expresses it like this:

And will this sovereign King
Of glory condescend?
And will He write His name
My Father and my Friend?
I love His name, I love His word,
Join all my powers to praise the Lord.

2. Because it is full of spiritual wisdom

What is wisdom? Who is the wise man? 'The fear of the Lord is the beginning of wisdom, and knowledge of the Holy One is understanding' (Proverbs 9:10). Plenty of people are clever and have great mental and intellectual powers; they can comprehend, invent, philosophize, and so on. But true wisdom is acquired only from God's Word, as God's Spirit teaches and instructs us. 'The man without the Spirit does not accept the things that come from the Spirit of God, for they are foolishness to him and he cannot understand them, because they are spiritually discerned' (1 Corinthians 2:14). So the psalmist can make the following statements:

'Your commands make me wiser than my enemies' (v.98).

'I have more insight than all my teachers,
        for I meditate on your statutes.
I have more understanding than the elders,
        for I obey your precepts' (vv.99-100).

'I have not departed from your laws,
        for you yourself have taught me' (v.102).

Here in God's Word we learn of His gracious character and purposes: what sin is in all its sinfulness, and the only way in which it may be pardoned; where true joy is to be found; how our heavenly Father undertakes for us all our days; how heaven is to be gained, and so on. Well may we say,

'All the days ordained for me
        were written in your book

before one of them came to be.
How precious to me are your thoughts, O God!
    How vast is the sum of them!'

(Psalm 139:16-17).

Or as that same psalm says,

'Such knowledge is too wonderful for me,
    too lofty for me to attain'

(Psalm 139:6).

3. Because it calls us to holiness

Do you recall the prayer of the Lord Jesus Christ for His church in John 17:17? He prayed, 'Sanctify them by the truth; your word is truth.' We not only learn in the Scriptures how to be converted from the paths of sin (being made 'wise for salvation through faith in Christ Jesus', 2 Timothy 3:15), but how to be vessels fit for the Master's use, men and women of God 'thoroughly equipped for every good work' (2 Timothy 3:17). Here, in the Word, the call to holiness is sounded, the paths to holiness are described and the helps to holiness are identified. 'It is God's will that you should be sanctified . . . For God did not call us to be impure, but to live a holy life. Therefore, he who rejects this instruction does not reject man but God, who gives you his Holy Spirit' (1 Thessalonians 4:3,7-8).

'I have kept my feet from every evil path
    so that I might obey your word' (v.101).

'I gain understanding from your precepts;
    therefore I hate every wrong path' (v.104).

So says the psalmist, for he knew that not only growth in knowledge, but growth in grace is promoted by God's Word — and we need both in vast measure! It was the prayer of Robert Murray M'Cheyne of Dundee: 'Lord, make me as holy as a pardoned sinner can ever be.' Is that our prayer too? M'Cheyne also remarked, 'It is not great talents God blesses so much as great likeness to Jesus. A holy minister is an awful weapon in the hand of God.' And, of course, what goes for ministers in that connection goes for every Christian.

4. Because its promises are so sweet

This is not the first time in our journey through Psalm 119 that we have made mention of God's promises, of which His Word is so abundantly full. Have you got 'a sweet tooth'? We all should have one for God's promises, says the psalmist: 'How sweet are your words to my taste, sweeter than honey to my mouth!' (v.103). They are tried, trusted and proved! Well did Joshua confess, 'You know with all your heart and soul that not one of all the good promises the Lord your God gave you has failed. Every promise has been fulfilled; not one has failed' (Joshua 23:14).

Only the believer has this spiritual taste, whatever the subject of the promises. Some of them assure us of His everlasting love; some breathe comfort into the daily conflicts of our Christian pilgrimage; some are like refreshing waters to tired and tempted souls; some display his divine and gracious sovereignty in choosing us, saving us and never letting us go. The range covered by the promises of God is, quite literally, breathtaking!

In chapter 11 I recorded A. W. Pink's description of God's promises as 'the outward testimonies of His heart', and so they are. Spurgeon says of them, 'They come from a great God, they come to great sinners, they work for us great results, and deal with great matters.' And, commenting on Peter's description of them as 'his very great and precious promises' (2 Peter 1:4), Spurgeon adds, 'Greatness and preciousness seldom go together, but in this instance they are united in an exceeding degree.'

Do you, as a Christian, love God's Word, not least because it abounds with the sweet promises of God, and do you make a proper use of these promises? What is that proper use of them? Let the apostle Paul answer: 'Since we have these promises, dear friends, let us purify ourselves from everything that contaminates body and spirit, perfecting holiness out of reverence for God' (AV, 'in the fear of God') (2 Corinthians 7:1).

'Your word is a lamp to my feet
   and a light for my path.
I have taken an oath and confirmed it,
   that I will follow your righteous laws.
I have suffered much;
   preserve my life, O Lord, according to your word.
Accept, O Lord, the willing praise of my mouth,
   and teach me your laws.
Though I constantly take my life in my hands,
   I will not forget your law.
The wicked have set a snare for me,
   but I have not strayed from your precepts.
Your statutes are my heritage for ever;
   they are the joy of my heart.
My heart is set on keeping your decrees
   to the very end'

(Psalm 119:105-112).

14.
Lighting-up time

Psalm 119:105-112

'Your word is a lamp to my feet and a light for my path' (v.105).

One of the most familiar verses of this psalm (or, for that matter, of the whole Bible) must surely be verse 105: 'Your word is a lamp to my feet and a light for my path.' It is a very important verse because it points us to the illumination, or instruction, of God's Word. It conveys a number of different ideas.

It conveys the idea of *'day and night'*, or all the time. Lamps are lit at night, and the light shines during the day. So there is in God's Word all that we need, all the time, in all the circumstances and changes of life — to instruct us, guide us, direct us, inform us, support us and do everything that is necessary for us. It is a most wonderful gift and provision from God.

It also conveys the idea of *'far and near'*, or everywhere. 'A lamp to my feet' shows me what is just in front of me, the things that are near at hand and of present or immediate concern. 'A light for my path' shines ahead, shows me where I am going (or ought to be going), keeps the goal in view and assures me that in the gracious purposes and providences of God my future is secure. God is over my life and directing my life today, and God will continually be over my life and directing my life. As Psalm 48:14 says, 'For this God is our God for ever and ever; he will be our guide even to the end.' Equally precious is Psalm 73:24: 'You guide me with your counsel, and afterwards you will take me into glory.'

Another idea conveyed here is that of *'general and particular'*, or everything. God's Word sets out the general course of life which we should pursue. It answers the questions, 'How should we then live?' (Ezekiel 33:10, AV) and 'What kind of people ought you to be?' (2 Peter 3:11). But that is not all: it also shows us how to conduct ourselves in specifics from day to day. There are both general principles and particular examples for us to learn and apply.

All of this, of course, presupposes the profound, enlightening work of God's Holy Spirit upon our minds, hearts and consciences; otherwise, however clear God's Word may be, we shall not grasp it, understand it, obey it or follow it. The hymn which, taking its cue from this verse, begins,

> Lamp of our feet, whereby we trace
> Our path when wont to stray,

goes on to say,

> Our guide and chart, wherein we read
> Of realms beyond the sky,

and concludes,

> Yet to unfold thy hidden worth,
> Thy mysteries to reveal,
> That Spirit who first gave thee forth,
> Thy volume must unseal.
>
> Lord, grant that we aright may learn
> The wisdom it imparts,
> And to its heavenly teaching turn,
> With simple, childlike hearts.

(Bernard Barton).

1. God's Word directs us into the right way

It directs us into the right way of salvation

We are living in days of tremendous confusion where the gospel is concerned. The reason for such confusion is, at root, quite simple to diagnose. In so many quarters and on so many sides the question is no longer asked: 'What does the

Scripture say?' (Romans 4:3); nor do we hear the cry: 'To the law and to the testimony! If they do not speak according to this word, they have no light of dawn' (Isaiah 8:20). In other words, many have abandoned the Scriptures, the Word of God, as the final, sufficient, infallible declaration of God, by which all doctrine (everything that is to be believed) and all practice (everything that is done) is to be tested and judged. It is no longer taken as the final arbiter. Much of the so-called church has cast it out and so there is no longer a clear note being sounded from the trumpet, so that the world is, of necessity, thrown into further confusion and unable to make head or tail (even if they wanted to) of what Christians really believe.

This applies particularly to the heart of the gospel itself — the way of salvation. When so many oft-quoted church leaders hold multi-faith services, attend multi-faith conferences and deny the absolute uniqueness and exclusiveness of the gospel, is it any wonder there is such turmoil?

Yet the Word of God is so very, very, plain: 'I, even I, am the Lord, and apart from me there is no saviour' (Isaiah 43:11). 'Jesus answered, "I am the way and the truth and the life. No one comes to the Father except through me"' (John 14:6). 'Salvation is found in no one else, for there is no other name under heaven given to men by which we must be saved' (Acts 4:12). 'For there is one God and one mediator between God and men, the man Christ Jesus, who gave himself as a ransom for all men' (1 Timothy 2:5-6).

It directs us into the right way of pleasing God

This is not something which we decide, or on which we make up our own minds. God sets out before us in His Word the things that are pleasing to Him and, equally, either explicitly or by implication, the things that are displeasing to Him. Again, the Word of God is so very, very plain, and there is no need whatever for all the confusion and the conflicting voices we hear both inside and outside the church, whether on general principles (such as, the need to obey God's law), or on specific examples (such as the sinfulness of homosexuality or the requirement for capital punishment to be the penalty for murder). Why is it that men would always rather debate an issue and come to their own conclusions (whether the view of the majority, or of a minority), than humble and submit themselves before the bar of the Word which God has spoken?

2. God's Word directs us away from the wrong way

It directs us away from every wrong way of salvation

Just as there is only *one right way* of salvation, into which God's Word directs the sinner (faith in Christ), so there are *many wrong ways* of salvation, and God's Word warns us against them and directs us away from them. 'There is a way that seems right to a man, but in the end it leads to death' (Proverbs 14:12). That was the text of Scripture which God used powerfully in the conviction and conversion of A. W. Pink, bringing him from wrong paths to the one right path for the salvation of his soul.

In particular, God's Word directs us right away from that most popular form of wrong ways — doing good, works of self-righteousness, trying to build up our own account of merit with God. The letter of Paul to the Galatians is particularly potent in this regard, with its insistence that 'By observing the law no one will be justified' (Galatians 2:16); the same verse makes plain the one sure way: 'We may be justified by faith in Christ and not by observing the law.'

It directs us away from every wrong way of sin and error

It puts, for example, a great stress on the need for purity of heart, mind, thought, speech and life. God's people are commanded to have nothing to with idolatry, strife, worldliness and suchlike. It exposes dangers such as legalism, antinomianism and perfectionism, which, at the risk of oversimplification, we could paraphrase as a life without the Spirit, a life without the law and a life without any sin — all of which are false doctrines and all of which are still prevalent today.

It directs us into the truth about Christ

Most importantly of all, the Scriptures direct us into the truth, and away from error, concerning the person and work of the Lord Jesus Christ. As John Newton observed so rightly,

> 'What think ye of Christ?' is the test
> To try both your state and your scheme;
> You cannot be right in the rest
> If you do not think rightly of Him.

3. God's Word directs us through the dark way

We can be tempted to say, 'My way is hidden from the Lord; my cause is disregarded by my God' (Isaiah 40:27), or to ask, 'Has God forgotten to be gracious?' or 'Is He not going to answer my prayer?' How can the Word of God be a lamp and a light to us in such circumstances? By recalling us to the crucial perspective of Isaiah 50:10:

> 'Who among you fears the Lord
>   and obeys the word of his servant?
> Let him who walks in the dark,
>   who has no light,
> trust in the name of the Lord
>   and rely on his God.'

Remember that the 'name' of the Lord is not just used for purposes of identification; it gathers together all that He is, all that He does and all that He promises — He who is the everlasting God, who never changes, and who, in the covenant of grace, is our God for ever. Where is all this displayed? In His Word!

How thankful we should be for God's Word, and how much more familiar we should be with it than we are!

It would be appropriate to close this section with this prayer of Charles Bridges: 'Lord! as every action of the day is a step to heaven, or hell — Oh! save me from ever turning my face away from the path, into which Thy word would guide me. Enable me to avail myself of its light, in the constant exercise of faith, prudence and simplicity.'

'I hate double-minded men,
   but I love your law.
You are my refuge and my shield;
   I have put my hope in your word.
Away from me, you evildoers,
   that I may keep the commands of my God!
Sustain me according to your promise, and I shall live;
   do not let my hopes be dashed.
Uphold me, and I shall be delivered;
   I shall always have regard for your decrees.
You reject all who stray from your decrees,
   for their deceitfulness is in vain.
All the wicked of the earth you discard like dross;
   therefore I love your statutes.
My flesh trembles in fear of you;
   I stand in awe of your laws'

(Psalm 119:113-120).

15.
All of grace

Psalm 119:113-120

'Sustain me according to your promise, and I shall live . . .
uphold me, and I shall be delivered' (vv.116-117).

The psalmist opens this fifteenth section of the psalm with a statement which in the NIV is translated, 'I hate double-minded men,' while in the AV it reads, 'I hate vain thoughts.' The truth of the matter is that this is the one and only occurrence anywhere in the Bible of the word translated either 'double-minded men' or 'vain thoughts'. Both translations seem valid. Certainly it appears that the word can be taken in terms of 'thoughts' (in connection with which different translators and commentators have rendered it, variously, 'crooked thoughts', 'wild imaginations', 'evil imaginations' and 'vain opinions'). But, equally, we may take it to refer to persons (and some of the translations that have been on offer this time include 'those that think vain thoughts', 'the unjust', 'the light-minded', 'doubtful men', 'wicked men', 'waverers', 'violent' or 'tumultuous men'). The word 'waverers' is an interesting one and conveys the same idea as the NIV's 'double- minded'. That is the translation that we shall pursue here.

Early on in his New Testament letter, James makes a remark about the double-minded man. He describes him as 'unstable in all he does', and 'like a wave of the sea, blown and tossed by the wind' (James 1:6-8). Here in Psalm 119, the psalmist is speaking of the same person. 'I hate double-minded men' is his strong way of expressing his own (and, for that matter, God's) utter abhorrence of double-mindedness — that spirit and attitude of wanting the best of both worlds, wavering between two opinions, and so having a divided heart and a distracted life. He goes on to characterize such folk as 'evildoers' (v.115), those 'who stray from [God's] decrees' (v.118), deceitful (v.118), and 'the wicked of the earth', whom God discards 'like dross' (v.119).

By way of contrast, the psalmist's great desire and longing is to be a stable man — steady, constant, firm, decided, uncompromising and abiding. In this section he draws our attention to some of the characteristics of such a believer, reminding us in so doing of several qualities which have already surfaced earlier in the psalm. The stable, or single-minded, man loves God's law (v.113), has put his hope in God's Word (v.114), keeps the commands of God (v.115), has regard and respect for God's decrees (v.117), loves God's statutes (v.119), trembles in fear of God and stands in awe of His laws (v.120).

But the question arises: how does he do this? Is it in his own strength? Is it by his own ability? Is it just by chance? If it is none of these things, then how is it? The psalmist does not tease us or leave us in the dark. He lets us into the secret, for the distinctive theme of these verses, the particular facet of God's Word that is set forth in this section is this: God Himself is the sustainer and upholder of all those who love His Word, keep His law and seek to pursue a single-minded course to His glory.

If we would make progress in our love for God's Word, our obedience to God's Word and our contending for God's Word, then two things must follow.

1. We are in continual need of God's sustaining grace

'Sustain me according to your promise, and I shall live' (v.116). The more mindful we are of our weakness, the more conscious we shall be of our need for God Himself to sustain us. This verb 'sustain' is a grand and embracing one. It comprises a whole cluster of thoughts and petitions: 'Bear my weight; keep me from falling; do not let me sink; enable me to last out; give me strength; encourage me; keep me going continually.' All of which is exactly what we need our gracious God to do for us!

Now let us see what the psalmist does and what we may do.

He pleads God's own promise! We can be sure that God will not fail or forsake us, for He has given us His word of promise. Our continuance, our stability and our endurance are grounded upon divine supports.

The apostle Paul was trained in this very school of being sustained by God's all-sufficient grace, according to God's own promise. He tells us about it in 2 Corinthians 12. Speaking of his 'thorn in the flesh', he writes this: 'Three times I pleaded with the Lord to take it away from me. But he said to me, "My grace is sufficient for you, for my power is made perfect in weakness." Therefore I will boast all the more gladly about my weaknesses, so that Christ's power may rest on me. That is why, for Christ's sake, I delight in weaknesses, in insults, in hardships, in persecutions, in difficulties. For when I am weak, then I am strong.'

All of this, of course, is very directly linked to that most blessed doctrine that we call the final perseverance, and final preservation, of the saints. Our God will not let us go. The darker the day, the fiercer the battle, the weaker we feel, the harder we find it, the nearer we are to collapse, then the more we need to remember the truths so well expressed in Toplady's hymn:

> The work which His goodness began,
> The arm of His strength will complete;
> His promise is Yea and Amen
> And never was forfeited yet.
> Things future, nor things that are now,
> Not all things below or above
> Can make Him His purpose forego
> Or sever my soul from His love.
>
> My name from the palms of His hands
> Eternity will not erase;
> Impressed on His heart it remains
> In marks of indelible grace;
> Yes, I to the end shall endure
> As sure as the earnest is given;
> More happy, but not more secure,
> The glorified spirits in heaven.

2. We are in continual need of God's upholding grace

'Uphold me, and I shall be delivered,' says the psalmist
(v.117). This is, in measure, an extension of the same
thought, though the Hebrew word for 'uphold' is sometimes
translated 'comfort' or 'refresh', and this draws from the commentator W. S. Plumer the excellent remark that 'The Lord
does not sustain His people merely by power, but gives them
cordials according to their faintness, and refreshments
according to their necessities.' Certainly the way the psalmist
puts these two verses (116 and 117) side by side reminds us
how we need constantly to be watching and praying. It literally is a case of 'I need Thee every hour, most gracious Lord.'

Charles Bridges puts it this way: 'I must send up one cry
after another into my Father's ear for the support of His
upholding grace. For not only the consciousness of my weakness, but the danger of the slippery path before me, reminds
me that the safety of every moment depends upon my upholding faithful God. The ways of temptation are so many and
imperceptible — the influence of it so appalling — the
entrance into it so deceitful . . . my own weakness and
unwatchfulness so unspeakable — that I can do nothing but
go on my way, praying at every step — "Hold Thou me up,
and I shall be safe".'

Our need of, and the divine assurance of, God's sustaining
and upholding grace is, so to speak, all gathered up together
in verse 114, where the psalmist testifies: 'You are my refuge
and shield; I have put my hope in your word.' Calvin remarks,
'True stability is to be found nowhere else but in the Word of
God; and no man can steadfastly lean upon it but he who is
strengthened by the power of the Holy Spirit.'

A nineteenth-century Christian, James Vaughan of
Brighton, (quoted in Spurgeon's *Treasury*), begins his
illuminating comment on this passage with the words: 'God's
methods of holding His people up are many.' Here are a few
extracts from what he wrote: 'Sometimes it is by the
preacher's word, when the word comes fitly spoken to the
heart and conscience . . . sometimes it is by the ordained
means and sacraments which His grace commanded . . . by
the efficacy of the Holy Scripture, when some passage in your
own room strikes the mind, just in season; or the stay of some

sweet promise comes in sustainingly to your spirit . . . Some-times by the ministration of angels . . . sometimes by putting you very low indeed, making you feel that the safe place is the valley. There is no elevation like the elevation of abasement. Sometimes by severe discipline to brace up the heart, and strengthen it, and make it independent of external things. Sometimes by heavy affliction, which is the grasp of His hand, that He may hold you tighter. Sometimes by putting into your heart to think the exact thing that you need — to pray the very prayer which He intends at the moment to grant. Sometimes by appearing to let you go and forsake you, while at the same time — like the Syro-Phœnician woman — He is giving you the wish to hold on that He may give you the more at the last.'

What, then, do we learn from this section of the psalm? Simply, yet profoundly, this: what is the secret of an unsteady, unstable, inconsistent walk? Neglecting to lean upon an almighty arm of divine resource. 'The arm of flesh will fail you — you dare not trust your own.' What, by way of contrast, is the secret of a steady, stable and single-minded Christian life of worship, devotion, service and usefulness? Leaning upon our covenant God who alone can keep us from falling into temptation, sin, error, mishap and disgrace. Plumer comments, 'Without divine grace assisting us, we are weak as water,' and Matthew Henry observes that 'We stand no longer than God holds us and go no further than He carries us.'

We could not really have a simpler or more exquisite lesson than this. God Himself is the sustainer and upholder of those who love His Word and keep His law. Yet we are so prone to forget it and so eager to go it alone, that there is hardly any lesson in the Christian life that it takes us longer to learn.

'I have done what is righteous and just;
   do not leave me to my oppressors.
Ensure your servant's well-being;
   let not the arrogant oppress me.
My eyes fail, looking for your salvation,
   looking for your righteous promise.
Deal with your servant according to your love
   and teach me your decrees.
I am your servant; give me discernment
   that I may understand your statutes.
It is time for you to act, O Lord;
   your law is being broken.
Because I love your commands
   more than gold, more than pure gold,
and because I consider all your precepts right,
   I hate every wrong path'

(Psalm 119:121-128).

16.
Time for action

Psalm 119:121-128

> *'It is time for you to act, O Lord; your law is being broken'* (v.126).

We often speak of the timelessness and relevance of God's Word, the Bible — and quite rightly so, of course. But sometimes, perhaps, we little realize just how timeless and how relevant it really is!

In Psalm 11:3 David asked the question: 'When the foundations are being destroyed, what can the righteous do?' This present section of Psalm 119 gives us the answer to the question. The key verse is verse 126, for the true answer to that question what the righteous can do is that they can call upon the Lord God to act! So the particular facet of the doctrine of Scripture set forth here is that the believer who loves God's Word is jealous for that Word to be upheld, it grieves him to see it broken and he calls urgently upon God to act.

In the opening verses of this section the psalmist declares that he has 'done what is righteous and just', and says that he is 'looking for your salvation, looking for your righteous promise'. Then at the end we get a glimpse of the 'jealousy' that inspires him: 'Your law is being broken . . . I love your commands . . . I consider all your precepts right, I hate every wrong path.' But the centrepiece is verse 126, where we find two things.

1. A realistic assessment

We shall start with the second part of the verse: 'Your law is being broken.' One of the more difficult things for true believers to do as we look around us, in the church and in the world, and consider what is going on, try to weigh it up, make some sense of it and come to some conclusions about it, is actually to make a *realistic* assessment of the situation. In one direction we can err on the side of unjustified optimism; in the other we can be unnecessarily pessimistic. To be realistic, to get the right balance, is what is so difficult, especially as our area of knowledge and our experience of history and current events (spiritual, political, moral, social, economic, etc.) is necessarily limited and restricted. Moreover, we are dependent for wider knowledge on various sources (news and media reports and so on), and they might on occasions be misleading, biased or positively wrong.

In general terms, and with many familiar and specific examples that we could give, we can say with confidence that what was for the psalmist a realistic assessment of the state of things in his own day is equally appropriate for our own: 'Your law is being broken.' That verb 'broken' is important. It can be rendered 'made void' and draws from Matthew Henry this comment: 'It is possible a godly man may sin *against* the commandment, but a wicked man would sin *away* the commandment, would repeal God's laws and enact his own lusts.' Charles Bridges remarks that men deny the law's power to rule and annul its power to punish. Is that not exactly what we see in our day? God's law and God's Word are not just sinned against, but actually sinned away! Man wants to repeal God's law and enact his own! So we find the state of things to be exactly as God says it will be in such circumstances and with such attitudes: 'The wrath of God is being revealed from heaven against all the godlessness and wickedness of men who suppress the truth by their wickedness' (Romans 1:18). 'But mark this: There will be terrible times in the last days . . . In fact, everyone who wants to live a godly life in Christ Jesus will be persecuted, while evil men and impostors will go from bad to worse, deceiving and being deceived' (2 Timothy 3:1,12-13).

What are some of the bold features of the present landscape in this respect?

1. The breakdown of law and order — the increase in riots, demonstrations, violence, commotion, terrorism, crime; the

abandonment of absolutes, as every man does what seems right in his own eyes.

2. Light views of the sanctity of life demonstrated in embryo research, abortion, surrogacy, younger and younger prostitution, the abandonment of capital punishment for murder, and the treatment of the elderly as 'disposable'.

3. The despising of discipline in schools and all the rising pressure against proper, biblical discipline in homes and families, as shown by the desire and attempts of various organizations and individuals to have corporal punishment outlawed by legislation.

4. The flouting of the Lord's Day.

5. The AIDS scourge; the flourishing of every perversion under the sun; evil being called good and good called evil; less and less firm moral stances being taken.

6. The continuing persecution of Christians, notwithstanding the remarkable changes and revolutions which have occurred in many parts of the world.

7. The almost wholesale failure of the established church and other denominational churches of our land to contend for the truth.

8. The nuclear threat.

9. Real political instability because of there being no real fear of God in the land. And so the list goes on.

We have to come before the Lord and say, 'Lord, your law is being broken, it is being made void, it is being cast down and cast aside, sinned against and sinned away. The sinfulness of sin is no longer regarded. There is no fear of God before men's eyes. Surely in one way and another you have raised up over us princes in your wrath.' That, surely, is a realistic assessment.

2. A heartfelt cry

Let us now turn to the first part of the verse: 'It is time for you to act, O Lord.' It is time for Jehovah to make bare His arm. It is time for the Lord God of hosts to declare Himself and display His sovereign power and glory. It is time, says Matthew Henry, 'for Thee, Lord . . . to do something for the effectual confutation of atheists and infidels and the silencing of those

that set their mouth against the heavens'. And he adds,
'God's time to work is when vice has become most daring and
the measure of iniquity is full.'

The One on whom the psalmist calls

He says, 'O Lord', using the name 'Jehovah', with all that it
implies of might, majesty, holiness, jealousy for God's glory,
strength, covenant grace and covenant faithfulness, and so on.

What he calls for

He calls for divine action, sovereign intervention and a
mighty demonstration of God's power. He says, in effect,
'Rise up, O Lord, and vindicate your own honour, glorify
your name, establish your law and in wrath remember
mercy.'

His own emotions

The psalmist demonstrates agony, agitation, anguish of soul
and great grief because God's law is being broken. The hotter
the opposition of God's enemies, and the greater and more
advanced their triumph seems to be, the more the true
believer's jealousy and zeal for God should grow and manifest
itself. Are we on the Lord's side? Then let us rise up in earnest, wrestling prayer and supplication, laying hold of the very
throne of God in passionate, heartfelt intercession for the
church, the nation and the world. (If we don't know how to
start, or want some clearer idea about how to go about it, or
what to say to God, then it would be a good idea to read
through Daniel 9 a few times.) We ought to be marked by a
holy indignation against sin, a fervent zeal for God's glory,
and to appeal from a clear conscience to God's faithfulness,
asking him to fulfil His promised judgements. Let us labour
and plead afresh for, and with, sinners in the matter of their
perishing souls, speaking urgently of the wonders of redeeming grace, as the day of judgement draws ever closer. Let us
also seek more grace for ourselves and for one another.
'Therefore put on the full armour of God, so that when the

day of evil comes, you may be able to stand your ground, and after you have done everything, to stand' (Ephesians 6:13).

To sum up, one old preacher, quoted, once again, in Spurgeon's *Treasury of David*, makes a fourfold division and application of this key text, as follows:

1. There are times when sin is specially active and dominant.

2. Such times reveal the dependence of the church upon God.

3. Such times awaken the desires of the church for the intervention of God.

4. Such times are the times when God does arise to plead His own cause.

And so we sing,

> God shall arise and by His might
> Put all His enemies to flight
> With shame and consternation.
> His haters, haughty though they be,
> Shall at His august presence flee
> In utter desolation:
>
> For when Jehovah shall appear,
> He shall consume, afar and near,
> All those that evil cherish.
> As smoke before His dreadful ire,
> As wax is melted by the fire
> So shall the wicked perish.
>
> Let God be praised with reverence deep;
> He daily comes our lives to steep
> In bounties freely given.
> God cares for us, our God is He;
> Who would not fear His majesty
> In earth as well as heaven?

Our God upholds us in the strife;
To us He grants eternal life
And saves from desolation.
He hears the needy when they cry,
He saves their souls when death draws nigh.
This God is our salvation!

(Essenburg).

'Your statutes are wonderful;
   therefore I obey them.
The unfolding of your words gives light;
   it gives understanding to the simple.
I open my mouth and pant,
   longing for your commands.
Turn to me and have mercy on me,
   as you always do to those who love your name.
Direct my footsteps according to your word;
   let no sin rule over me.
Redeem me from the oppression of men,
   that I may obey your precepts.
Make your face shine upon your servant
   and teach me your decrees.
Streams of tears flow from my eyes,
   for your law is not obeyed'

(Psalm 119:129-136).

17.
God's wonderful Word

Psalm 119:129-136

'*Your statutes are wonderful; therefore I obey them*' (v.129).

What is the psalmist doing in this seventeenth section of the psalm? We can set it out like this:

1. He praises God for His Word (vv.129-130).
2. He shows his affection and desire for God's Word (vv.131-132).
3. He prays for divine grace to keep God's Word (vv.133-135).
4. He mourns on account of those who disobey God's Word (v.136).

Let us focus our attention on verse 129, from which we may learn just how wonderful God's Word is. 'Your statutes [AV, 'testimonies'] are wonderful,' says the psalmist to God. They are wonderful in and of themselves, whether people think so or not. In that vital sense, God's Word is not affected one jot by people's attitudes and reactions, unlike the value of the pound, or its position in relation to the American dollar or German mark! But God's Word is especially wonderful to the believer. Spurgeon says, 'Those who know [it] best wonder at [it] most. It is wonderful that God should have borne testimony at all to sinful men, and more wonderful still that His testimony should be of such a character — so clear, so full, so gracious, so mighty.'

Let us consider some of the ways in which God's Word is wonderful to the believer, in the hope that each of them will find a resounding echo in our own souls!

1. Its origin and authority

Someone has written, 'The Bible itself is an astonishing and astounding miracle.' Amen! So it is! And that is true in several ways.

Its divine authorship

It is the Word of God and not the word of man. The two classic texts in this respect are 2 Timothy 3:16 and 2 Peter 1:21: '*All Scripture is God-breathed* and is useful for teaching, rebuking, correcting and training in righteousness.' 'For prophecy [Scripture] never had its origin in the will of man, but *men spoke from God* as they were carried along by the Holy Spirit.'

Strictly speaking, it is always more proper and appropriate to say that we come *under* God's Word, rather than *to* it or *around* it, for only that word 'under' conveys the sense of our being captive to its, and so to God's authority.

Its rich diversity

It was written portion by portion, book by book, over the course of many centuries, in different languages, by men of the most opposite tempers, talents and circumstances, and is cast in many varied forms and styles, including poetry, historical narrative, prophecy, apocalyptic imagery and so on.

Its accuracy and relevance

It is absolutely without error, contradiction or any redundant, irrelevant material.

Its marvellous preservation

Over the years people have sought to burn it, destroy it, alter it, deny it and do all manner of grievous things to it, and they still do! However, the glorious fact of the matter is well expressed in Isaiah 40:8: 'The grass withers and the flowers fall, but the Word of our God stands for ever.'

2. Its fulness and depth

Where do you begin to describe its contents? There are depths and heights, and breadths and lengths, of mystery, wisdom and glory here which are just not found anywhere else.

Here are just a few of the glorious truths contained in it for our meditation.

The doctrine of creation

'By the word of the Lord were the heavens made . . . For he spoke, and it came to be; he commanded, and it stood firm' (Psalm 33:6,9).

The character of God

'Oh, the depth of the riches of the wisdom and knowledge of God! How unsearchable his judgements, and his paths beyond tracing out!' (Romans 11:33).

The incarnation

'The Word became flesh and made his dwelling among us. We have seen his glory, the glory of the One and Only, who came from the Father, full of grace and truth' (John 1:14).

God's electing grace

'For he chose us in him [Christ] before the creation of the world to be holy and blameless in his sight' (Ephesians 1:4).

Heaven and hell

'His winnowing fork in his hand to clear his threshing-floor and to gather the wheat into his barn, but he will burn up the chaff with unquenchable fire' (Luke 3:17).

If it is a problem to know where to begin, once you have begun, where do you end? Charles Bridges comments that God's Word 'lays open to the heaven-taught soul what "eye hath not seen, nor ear heard, neither hath it entered into the heart of man" (1 Corinthians 2:9)', and he goes on to speak of 'the stupendous discoveries of the sacred book, that bow the humble and reflecting mind to the confession — "Thy testimonies are wonderful."'

In all of this it can both satisfy the deepest minds and yet be grasped by the simplest, when the Holy Spirit of God is our Teacher.

3. Its focus upon Christ

'These are the Scriptures that testify about me,' says the Lord Jesus Christ (John 5:39). Christ describes the great central ministry of the Holy Spirit in the following terms: 'He will guide you into all truth. He will not speak on his own . . . He will bring glory to me by taking from what is mine and making it known to you. All that belongs to the Father is mine. That is why I said the Spirit will take from what is mine and make it known to you' (John 16:13-15). The Bible is full of Christ from first to last. It draws continual straight lines to Him. The request of the Greeks who came to the disciples asking, 'Sir . . . we would like to see Jesus' (John 12:21), expresses the supreme desire of the true believer, as he or she approaches God's Word. Christ's own name is 'Wonderful' (Isaiah 9:6), so it is not surprising that the Word which testifies of Him is wonderful too!

The Old Testament ceremonial law is wonderful, especially in the way in which it sets forth the mystery of our redemption by the blood of Christ through its familiar types and symbols. The law of God is wonderful, not least in its task as a 'schoolmaster' to bring us to Christ (Galatians 3:24, AV). The prophecies of Scripture are wonderful, especially in the way so many of them deal very precisely with the person and work of Christ. The whole of the New Testament abounds with him and the fulness there is in Him alone of salvation, eternal life, holiness and glory.

4. Its wide-ranging power

Here are just a few examples of what I mean by this:

1. The power of God's Word, as it is blessed and pressed home by the Holy Spirit, to terrify, humble, convict and enlighten the sinner. In this connection, notice verse 130, which says, 'The unfolding [AV, 'entrance'] of your words gives light.'

2. The power of God's Word to awaken, draw, convict of, and instruct in, the truth.

3. The power of God's Word to elevate, comfort, strengthen, console and bless.

4. The power of God's Word to expose, transform, quicken and give life.

This is another of those lists which could very easily go on and on! Anne Steele expresses it this way:

Father of mercies, in Thy word
What endless glory shines!
For ever be Thy name adored
For these celestial lines.

Here springs of consolation rise
To cheer the fainting mind,
And thirsty souls receive supplies,
And sweet refreshment find.

Here the Redeemer's welcome voice
Spreads heavenly peace around;
And life and everlasting joys
Attend the blissful sound.

Oh, may these hallowed pages be
My ever dear delight!
And still new beauties may I see,
And still increasing light.

Divine Instructor, gracious Lord,
Be Thou for ever near;
Teach me to love Thy sacred Word,
And view my Saviour here.

If ever there was a day when all of this needed to be emphasized, surely it is now! What should be our response to the wonderful Word of God?

1. We are to bless and praise God for His Word. Let's ask ourselves, honestly, when we last did that.

2. We are to make the daily reading and study of it our discipline and delight, and never (except for the most genuine reasons on earth) absent ourselves from the preaching of it. Charles Bridges writes, 'Let us not enter into the "testimonies" as a dry task, or an ordinary study; but let us concentrate our minds, our faith, humility and prayer in a more devoted contemplation of them. Every such exercise will extend our view of those parts with which we had conceived ourselves to be competently acquainted: opening a new field of wonders on every side, far beyond our present contracted apprehensions.'

3. We should seek wisdom from God to know whom we should invite to hear the preaching of the Word, and then wait patiently for it to take its full effect upon their souls.

4. We are to contend earnestly and gladly, yet in a gracious manner, for God's Word against all comers.

5. We should count God's Word exceedingly precious. Henry Martyn once wrote, 'What do I not owe to the Lord for permitting me to take a part in the translation of His Word? Never did I see such wonders and wisdom and love in the blessed book, as since I have been obliged to study every expression; and it is a delightful reflection that death cannot deprive us of the pleasure of studying its mysteries.'

6. We must seek to obey God's Word at all times. For if God's Word is wonderful, it must be believed; and where it is believed, it must be obeyed. The psalmist says, 'Your statutes are wonderful; *therefore I obey them.*'

'Righteous are you, O Lord,
  and your laws are right.
The statutes you have laid down are righteous;
  they are fully trustworthy.
My zeal wears me out,
  for my enemies ignore your words.
Your promises have been thoroughly tested,
  and your servant loves them.
Though I am lowly and despised,
  I do not forget your precepts.
Your righteousness is everlasting
  and your law is true.
Trouble and distress have come upon me,
  but your commands are my delight.
Your statutes are for ever right;
  give me understanding that I may live'
                              (Psalm 119:137-144).

18.
A righteous God and a righteous Word

Psalm 119:137-144

> *'Righteous are you, O Lord, and your laws are right. The statutes you have laid down are righteous; they are fully trustworthy' (vv.137-138).*

The particular facet of the doctrine of God's Word which is highlighted in this section stands out straight away. You cannot miss it. We may call it the righteousness of God's Word.

'Your laws are right' (v.137).
'The statutes you have laid down are righteous;
    they are fully trustworthy' (v.138).
'Your promises have been thoroughly tested' (v.140).
'. . . your law is true' (v.142).
'Your statutes are for ever right' (v.144).

In highlighting this magnificent theme, we find the psalmist engaging in a very right and proper activity, and doing something which we ought to do ourselves. He argues from what God Himself is like, to what the things, ways and gifts of God are like. As an example of this, let us take verse 137:

1. What God Himself is like: 'Righteous are you, O Lord.'
2. What God's Word is like: 'Your laws are right.'
There is something very similar in verse 142:
1. What God Himself is like: 'Your righteousness is everlasting.'
2. What God's Word is like: 'Your law is true.'

Do you see the way in which the psalmist is proceeding?

Since God Himself is righteous, everything that proceeds from God must be righteous — in this case, especially, His Word. What does it mean to say that God is righteous? It includes the following: He is right, true, pure, holy, trustworthy, just, unchanging, unalterable, dependable, full of integrity, and so on. Since what is true of God Himself is true of the Word that has proceeded from His mind and His mouth, God's Word is also right, true, pure, holy, trustworthy, just, unchanging, unalterable, dependable, full of integrity, and so on.

In the same way, since God Himself is everlasting, so is His Word. The statement in verse 142 about God Himself, 'Your righteousness is everlasting,' leads to the declaration about God's Word in verse 144: 'Your statutes are for ever right.'

J. Graham Miller sums it all up in these words: 'God's Word, like Himself, is righteous. All that He has spoken is true to what He is in His own incorruptible integrity and truth. Because God is not subject to change and decay His Word is clothed with the same timeless quality.' He adds, 'The neglect and rejection of God's Word is a commentary on man's hostile heart, not upon God's timeless Word.'

What I want to do as we look at this section is to let the Word of God speak for itself, so that we might be impressed with the weight and the truth and the force of its own testimony. The divisions are suggested by an outline on verse 137 by George Rogers, one-time principal of the Pastors' College which Spurgeon established in London.

1. God's Word is righteous in its commands

'So then, the law is holy, and the commandment is holy, righteous and good' (Romans 7:12).

'And God spoke all these words: I am the Lord your God, who brought you out of Egypt, out of the land of slavery. You shall have no other gods before me. You shall not make for yourself an idol in the form of anything in heaven above or on the earth beneath or in the waters below. You shall not bow down to them or worship them . . . You shall not misuse the name of the Lord your God . . . Remember the Sabbath day by keeping it holy . . . Honour your father and your mother

. . . You shall not commit murder. You shall not commit adultery. You shall not steal. You shall not give false testimony against your neighbour. You shall not covet . . .' (Exodus 20:1- 17).

'Jesus replied: "'Love the Lord your God with all your heart and with all your soul and with all your mind.' This is the first and greatest commandment. And the second is like it: 'Love your neighbour as yourself.' All the Law and the Prophets hang on these two commandments"' (Matthew 22:37-40).

2. God's Word is righteous in its warnings

'The soul who sins is the one who will die' (Ezekiel 18:4).

'All who rely on observing the law are under a curse, for it is written: "Cursed is everyone who does not continue to do everything written in the Book of the Law"' (Galatians 3:10).

'The Lord will not hold anyone guiltless who misuses his name' (Exodus 20:7).

'How shall we escape if we ignore such a great salvation?' (Hebrews 2:3).

'It is a dreadful thing to fall into the hands of the living God' (Hebrews 10:31).

'So, because you are lukewarm — neither hot nor cold — I am about to spit you out of my mouth' (Revelation 3:16).

'There is a way that seems right to a man, but in the end it leads to death' (Proverbs 14:12).

'Not everyone who says to me, "Lord, Lord," will enter the kingdom of heaven, but only he who does the will of my Father who is in heaven. Many will say to me on that day, "Lord, Lord, did we not prophesy in your name, and in your name drive out demons and perform many miracles?" Then I will tell them plainly, "I never knew you. Away from me, you evildoers"' (Matthew 7:21-23).

3. God's Word is righteous in its providences

'But Joseph said to them, "Don't be afraid. Am I in the place of God? You intended to harm me, but God intended it for good to accomplish what is now being done, the saving of many lives' (Genesis 50:19-20).

'Endure hardship as discipline; God is treating you as sons. For what son is not disciplined by his father?' (Hebrews 12:7).

'Consider it pure joy, my brothers, whenever you face trials of many kinds, because you know that the testing of your faith develops perseverance. Perseverance must finish its work so that you may be mature and complete, not lacking anything' (James 1:2-4).

'Simon, Simon, Satan has asked to sift you as wheat. But I have prayed for you, Simon, that your faith may not fail. And when you have turned back, strengthen your brothers' (Luke 22:31-32).

4. God's Word is righteous in its judgements

'Far be it from you to do such a thing — to kill the righteous with the wicked, treating the righteous and the wicked alike. Far be it from you! Will not the Judge of all the earth do right?' (Genesis 18:25).

'The word of God is living and active. Sharper than any double-edged sword, it penetrates even to dividing soul and spirit, joints and marrow; it judges the thoughts and attitudes of the heart. Nothing in all creation is hidden from God's sight. Everything is uncovered and laid bare before the eyes of him to whom we must give account' (Hebrews 4:12-13).

'When he opened the fifth seal, I saw under the altar the souls of those who had been slain because of the word of God and the testimony they had maintained. They called out in a loud voice, "How long, Sovereign Lord, holy and true, until you judge the inhabitants of the earth and avenge our blood?"' (Revelation 6:9-10).

5. God's Word is righteous in its promises

'Come to me, all you who are weary and burdened, and I will give you rest' (Matthew 11:28).

'All that the Father gives me will come to me, and whoever comes to me I will never drive away' (John 6:37).

'Jesus said to her, "I am the resurrection and the life. He who believes in me will live, even though he dies; and whoever lives and believes in me will never die. Do you believe this?"' (John 11:25-26).

'Therefore tell the people: This is what the Lord Almighty says: "Return to me," declares the Lord Almighty, "and I will return to you," says the Lord Almighty' (Zechariah 1:3).

'My God will meet all your needs according to his glorious riches in Christ Jesus' (Philippians 4:19).

'At that time men will see the Son of Man coming in clouds with great power and glory. And he will send his angels and gather his elect from the four winds, from the ends of the earth to the ends of the heavens' (Mark 13:26-27).

Our psalmist was able to testify from his own personal experience, 'Your promises have been thoroughly tested, and your servant loves them' (v.40). And in verse 143 the dark cloud of the first half, 'Trouble and distress have come upon me,' is balanced by the silver lining of the second part: 'But your commands are my delight.' The Word of God is the believer's delight even when trouble and distress come upon him. How kind and gracious of our God that He has so framed His Word to this end, and how precious that we can resort to it with absolute confidence at such times!

> How firm a foundation, ye saints of the Lord,
> Is laid for your faith in His excellent Word!
> What more can He say than to you He hath said,
> You who unto Jesus for refuge have fled?
>
> 'Fear not, I am with thee, Oh, be not dismayed;
> I, I am thy God, and will still give thee aid:
> I'll strengthen thee, help thee, and cause thee to stand,
> Upheld by My righteous, omnipotent hand.'

'I call with all my heart; answer me, O Lord,
    and I will obey your decrees.
I call out to you; save me
    and I will keep your statutes.
I rise before dawn and cry for help;
    I have put my hope in your word.
My eyes stay open through the watches of the night,
    that I may meditate on your promises.
Hear my voice in accordance with your love;
    preserve my life, O Lord, according to your laws.
Those who devise wicked schemes are near,
    but they are far from your law.
Yet you are near, O Lord,
    and all your commands are true.
Long ago I learned from your statutes
    that you established them to last for ever'
                                            (Psalm 119:145-152).

19.
Together again

Psalm 119:145-152

> *'I call with all my heart; answer me, O Lord, and I will obey your decrees'* (v.145).

Certain things belong together by association — like mince and dumplings, Laurel and Hardy, sunshine and showers. Far more seriously, the Word and prayer make a classic pair. Earlier on in the psalm (verses 73-80, see chapter 10) the theme was prayer stirred up by God's Word. Now in the present section the Word and prayer are thrown together again. What a natural combination they make — whether in the secret place, at family worship or in the church of Christ!

There are three profitable lines to explore here concerning this pairing of the Word and prayer.

1. The Word directs us to the God to whom we pray

Three times in these eight verses the psalmist cries, 'O Lord', reminding us each time that our God is personal. The psalmist is not addressing 'someone out there', or uttering words which, for all he knows, are just 'into the air'. He is praying to God, to the Lord, to Jehovah. He is addressing the God who is real, mighty, holy and glorious. He is dealing in prayer with the gracious and faithful God of the covenant. God is personal. God has established a relationship with the psalmist that is intimate and familiar. We may even say, they know each other. They are not strangers.

This matter of 'relationship' in prayer is tremendously important. Guy Appéré draws this out near the beginning of

his helpful little book on prayer, *Dialogue with God*. There
are, he reminds us, three aspects to the relationship involved
whenever the Christian prays. There is the relationship of the
creature before his Creator, the relationship of the sinner
before the just and holy God, and the relationship of the son
before his Father. The first, he says, arouses in our minds a
respectful fear of God; the second gives rise in our souls to the
feeling of condemnation, while the third brings the simple
and joyful assurance with which the Father's love fills the
hearts of His children. Appéré concludes the chapter in this
way: 'The feeling of weakness and dependence of the creature in the presence of his Creator, the sense of unworthiness
of the sinner before the threefold holiness of God, the feeling
of joy and freedom of the son before his Father, these are the
three conditions needed for a right attitude in prayer.' So they
are, and the psalmist knew it!

Looking at each of the three times that the psalmist addresses God in this section, we find that each one gives us a
different aspect of the God to whom we pray.

The Lord who answers

'I call with all my heart; answer me, O Lord' (v.145). Not only
does God answer; He is more ready to hear us than we are to
pray. He even says, 'Before they call I will answer; while they
are still speaking I will hear' (Isaiah 65:24). Moreover, He 'is
able to do immeasurably more than all we ask or imagine'
(Ephesians 3:20). This, surely, is the great and necessary spur
to, and warrant for, prayer — that God does and will hear us
and that He will answer us. This is something the saints of
God have proved continually, not least in the darkest days
and in the midst of the most dire experiences. To read John
G. Paton's autobiography, relating his days as a missionary to
the New Hebrides (in the South Seas), is to be reminded of
this again and again. Wasn't this, indeed, one of the
mainstays of the Saviour's own prayer life? Remember how
He prayed at the tomb of Lazarus: 'Father, I thank you that
you have heard me. I knew that you always hear me, but I said
this for the benefit of the people standing here . . .' (John
11:41-42).

The Lord who acts

'Hear my voice in accordance with your love; preserve my life, O Lord, according to your laws' (v.149). How much we need this divine quickening! Think of the promise of Isaiah 44:3, where God says,

> 'For I will pour water on the thirsty land,
>   and streams on the dry ground;
> I will pour out my Spirit on your offspring,
>   and my blessing on your descendants.'

The Lord who is near

> 'Those who devise wicked schemes are near,
>   but they are far from your law.
> Yet you are near, O Lord'
>
> (vv.150-151).

I came upon a treatment of the thought expressed here which set it out like this: 'Man is near to harass; God is near to help. Man is near to hurt; God is near to protect. Man is near to discourage; God is near to comfort. Man is near to tempt to sin; God is near to save from sin. Man is near to cast doubts; God is near to resolve doubts. Man is near to drag down to the world, flesh and devil; God is near to lift up to heavenly things, where Christ sits at His right hand. Man is near to kill; God is near to give life and immortality.'

2. The Word stirs us up to earnestness before God

I dare say most of us know something of what the hymn-writer describes in these familiar words:

> I often say my prayers,
> But do I ever pray?
> And do the wishes of my heart
> Go with the words I say?

I may as well kneel down
And worship gods of stone,
As offer to the living God
A prayer of words alone.

For words without the heart
The Lord will never hear;
Nor will He to those lips attend
Whose prayers are not sincere.

Lord, teach me what I need
And teach me how to pray;
And do not let me seek Thy grace
Not meaning what I say.

                                                                (John Burton).

If that is so, we are in great need of spiritual quickening and
divine assistance to pray really, fervently and spiritually.
Here, very especially, the Word of God (read, meditated
upon and preached) can be such a help in fuelling our earnest-
ness. This is not a new thought in Psalm 119, but it is worth
pursuing it a little more. We shall notice three things from this
section.

Calling with all our hearts

This comes through in verses 145 and 146: 'I call with all my
heart . . . I call out to you.' Stretched, passionate, pleading,
energetic praying is in view here. Our God desires it from us.
He delights in it. Prayers of our lips alone are a mockery
before Him. He does not delight in lip-service; He would
have our hearts. We must engage the whole of our minds,
hearts, emotions, wills and voices in the work of prayer.

Rising before dawn

Maybe this is not something that many of us excel at. While
there is always the danger of an unhelpful, and unbiblical,
legalism with regard to the relative merits of this or that hour
for prayer, yet we cannot escape a distinct emphasis in various
Scriptures upon seeking the Lord early in the day. Certainly

this was the Saviour's frequent practice, of which Mark 1:35 is a typical example: 'Very early in the morning, while it was still dark, Jesus got up, left the house and went off to a solitary place, where he prayed.' Is this a detail in which we seek to be Christ-like? Since the Lord's mercies are new every morning, it is appropriate that our prayers to Him should be the same. Matthew Henry observes that 'If our thoughts in the morning are of God, they will help to keep us in His fear all the day long.' (In *Directions for Daily Communion with God* Matthew Henry shows us how to begin, how to spend, and how to end each day with Him.)

Meditating during the night

Not only, says the psalmist, do 'I rise before dawn and cry for help' (v.147), but 'My eyes stay open through the watches of the night' (v.148). For what purpose? To what profit? 'That I may meditate on your promises.' One of the contributors to the *Preacher's Homiletic Commentary* has some thoughtful observations on this verse. Nightly meditation will prepare us for daily obedience. Nightly remembrance of God will stimulate daily thoughts about Him. Nightly thanksgiving will be a healthy preparation for the recognition of daily mercies.

3. The Word leads us into sober resolutions towards God

One of the repeated thrusts of this whole psalm has been that the Word of God demands our practical response. We do not just read it. We do not come to it as spectators. We are not unrelated to it. It is God's dynamic Word. And as this nineteenth section of the psalm closes, this is the theme once again. Three things are in view by way of the Word of God having a vital effect upon us, as God's people, to the glory of God in our lives.

It prompts obedience

'I will obey your decrees . . . and I will keep your statutes' (vv.145,146).

It engages our hope or trust

'I have put my hope in your word' (v.147).

It fires assurance

> 'Yet you are near, O Lord,
>   and all your commands are true.
> Long ago I learned from your statutes
>   that you established them to last for ever'
>
> (vv.151-152).

'Look upon my suffering and deliver me,
   for I have not forgotten your law.
Defend my cause and redeem me;
   preserve my life according to your promise.
Salvation is far from the wicked,
   for they do not seek out your decrees.
Your compassion is great, O Lord;
   preserve my life according to your laws.
Many are the foes who persecute me,
   but I have not turned from your statutes.
I look on the faithless with loathing,
   for they do not obey your word.
See how I love your precepts;
   preserve my life, O Lord, according to your love.
All your words are true
   all your righteous laws are eternal'

(Psalm 119:153-160).

20.
Keeping an eye

Psalm 119:153-160

*'Your compassion is great, O Lord; preserve my life according
to your laws'* (v.156).

It may be that when we set out with these brief studies (or
even 'hors-d'œuvres'!) on Psalm 119, some readers wondered
if there really could be as many as twenty-two different facets
to God's Word. Well, here is yet another of them: the God of
the Word. God is not only the Author of the Bible; He has
given it to us as the vehicle whereby He reveals Himself, man-
ifests Himself and makes Himself known to us. The Bible is
the Word of God. He is the God of the Word — the God
whose Word it is, and who declares Himself in it. He reveals
Himself here for our knowledge and our profit.

So let me ask a question: what is the most important thing
for each of us in life — and not only in life but for all eternity?
It is this: to know God. One of the most famous questions
(probably the most famous) in the Westminster Shorter
Catechism is the one with which it begins:

'Question: What is the chief end of man?
Answer: Man's chief end is to glorify God, and to enjoy
Him for ever.'

That is not how a vast number of people would see it, nor
the answer they would give to the question, of course; but that
is how God has purposed it. That is why He created man in
the very beginning, and that is why He is pleased to give to
each of us life and breath and being — so that we should
glorify and enjoy Him. But in order to do this, in order that we

should glorify and enjoy God, we need to know Him.

'This is what the Lord says:

"Let not the wise man boast of his wisdom
   or the strong man boast of his strength
   or the rich man boast of his riches,
but let him who boasts boast about this:
   that he understands and knows me,
that I am the Lord, who exercises kindness,
   justice and righteousness on earth,
   for in these I delight,"
declares the Lord'

(Jeremiah 9:23-24).

What does the Lord Jesus Christ say about eternal life in John 17:3? 'Now this is eternal life: that they may know you, the only true God, and Jesus Christ, whom you have sent.' Do you know God?

Who is God? What is God like? How does God act? These are questions which can only be answered from the Word, and in this twentieth section of the psalm the psalmist (to use Matthew Henry's phrase) 'has an eye' to various characteristics and attributes of the God of the Word. As we notice them, we need to turn them into praise and prayer.

1. God's compassion

When the psalmist says in verse 153, 'Look upon my suffering and deliver me,' he means, 'Take it into your thoughts, along with all the details and circumstances of it. Please do not sit by as if you were unconcerned.' Then, in verse 156, he makes a direct reference to God's compassion (AV, 'tender mercies'): 'Your compassion is great, O Lord.'

God is the compassionate God. He is full of compassion. There is absolutely no sense in which God just stands by unfeelingly, unconcerned and uncaring, (or unknowing), although He would still have us plead our need before Him, and 'put Him in remembrance' of how it is with us. This is not because He would not know otherwise, nor because He might forget, nor because He needs to have His arm twisted; but in order to develop in us a spirit of dependence upon Him as our God and Father. David Dickson says, 'As the mercies of the Lord, which are the fountain of all the benefits the believer asks, are very excellent in themselves, so are they in the estimation of the believer, when he looks upon them; they are many and mother-like, tender and great.'

Particularly precious is David's testimony in Psalm 40:17:

> 'Yet I am poor and needy;
>   may the Lord think of me.
> You are my help and my deliverer;
>   O my God, do not delay.'

This leads us straight on to our next point.

2. God's power

Why does the psalmist ask God to look upon his suffering? In order to deliver him! He says so: 'Deliver me' (v.153), 'Preserve my life' (v.159). Matthew Henry comments, 'God has promised deliverance and we may pray for it, with submission to His will and with regard to His glory, that we may serve Him the better.' And we have a most magnificent promise from God to this very point: 'And God is faithful; he will not let you be tempted [tried] beyond what you can bear. But when you are tempted, he will also provide a way out so that you can stand up under it' (1 Corinthians 10:13).

We have every reason for confidence that God sees all our troubles and knows all our fears, yet as David Dickson says, 'We can hardly rest satisfied till He by real effect makes it evident that He pities us in our affliction, and delivers us out of it.' And when He does deliver us, what overwhelmingly happy and blessed days we enjoy, full of relief and praise!

> His love in time past
> Forbids me to think
> He'll leave me at last
> In trouble to sink;

Each sweet Ebenezer
I have in review
Confirms His good pleasure
To help me quite through.

Since all that I meet
Shall work for my good,
The bitter is sweet,
The medicine is food;
Though painful at present,
'Twill cease before long;
And then, Oh how pleasant
The conqueror's song!

(John Newton).

3. God's righteousness

'Defend my cause and redeem me,' cries the psalmist (v.154). In this request it is on God's righteousness that his eye focuses. The psalmist has a cause to plead. He is in difficulty. He is under pressure. He had mentioned earlier in the psalm, among other things, how wicked men were wronging him without any cause. He was in something of a tight corner.

So what did he do? He took his cause to the covenant God, to whom he belonged. There is a sense here of God being our Advocate or Counsel, and us His clients, if we may put it like that. He submitted himself to God's wisdom and God's judgement, and was quite sure in his mind and heart that all would consequently be well. He felt, no doubt, like Abraham of old, who expressed his own firm confidence in God with the question: 'Will not the Judge of all the earth do right?' (Genesis 18:25).

This is very important in the Christian life. God is righteous. He loves what is right and He hates what is wrong. He is the God of justice, not of injustice. He is not some cold and dispassionate Judge. He particularly loves to plead and undertake for His people's cause. Why? Because it is His own cause! His name, His glory, His honour, His gospel are all bound up in it. The psalmist 'has a just cause, but his adversaries were many and mighty, and he was in danger of being run down by them; he therefore begs of God to clear his integrity and silence their false accusations. If God will not plead His people's cause, who will?' (Matthew Henry).

The beauty of all this, as we come to God in this manner, (whatever it may be that is affecting us, being said about us, or being done to us) is that the Lord our God never loses a case. However, we must remember that in some cases we may have to wait patiently for the last day for our vindication. But that day is sure to come! We must seek grace to heed the counsel of the psalmist David, and follow the example of the Saviour, our Lord Jesus Christ:

> 'Commit your way to the Lord;
>   trust in Him and He will do this:
> He will make your righteousness shine like the dawn,
>   the justice of your cause like the noonday sun.
> Be still before the Lord and wait patiently for him;
>   do not fret when men succeed in their ways,
>   when they carry out their wicked schemes.
>
> Refrain from anger and turn from wrath;
>   do not fret — it leads only to evil.
> For evil men will be cut off,
>   but those who hope in the Lord will inherit the land'
>   (Psalm 37:5-9).

Make a point of reading through the whole psalm more than once!

'But how is it to your credit if you receive a beating for doing wrong and endure it? But if you suffer for doing good and you endure it, this is commendable before God. To this you were called, because Christ suffered for you, leaving you an example, that you should follow in his steps. "He committed no sin, and no deceit was found in his mouth." When they hurled their insults at him, he did not retaliate; when he suffered, he made no threats. Instead, he entrusted himself to him who judges justly' (1 Peter 2:20-23).

Keeping an eye upon the character of God is a fundamental and constant necessity for the child of God and the church of God. We so easily find our eyes straying just about

everywhere else, and then we wonder why we become so fear-
ful and discomforted. You may like to work out for yourself
some further thoughts along the same lines: what else does
the psalmist keep an eye out for? We could mention God's
quickening (vv.154,156), God's name (v.157-158 — because
of those who hate Him and his people) and God's faithfulness
(vv.159-160 — in terms of His love and His eternal Word of
truth). We shall not move too far away from considerations of
the character of God as we continue into the next section of
the psalm.

'Rulers persecute me without cause,
  but my heart trembles at your word.
I rejoice in your promise
  like one who finds great spoil.
I hate and abhor falsehood
  but I love your law.
Seven times a day I praise you
  for your righteous laws.
Great peace have they who love your law,
  and nothing can make them stumble.
I wait for your salvation, O Lord,
  and I follow your commands.
I obey your statutes,
  for I love them greatly.
I obey your precepts and your statutes,
  for all my ways are known to you'

(Psalm 119:161-168).

21.
RSVP

Psalm 119:161-168

> *'I rejoice in your promise like one who finds great spoil'* (v.162).

Right at the beginning, when introducing the psalm, I remarked that one commentator, Charles Bridges in fact, described Psalm 119 as 'twenty-two pearls upon one string'. Still on the theme of strings, as we come to the last-but-one section of the psalm, J. Graham Miller (in his book of daily Bible Readings, *The Treasury of His Promises*) remarks that 'In these eight verses we hear sweet music played upon an instrument of seven strings . . . These seven strings spell out the perfection of the Word in its satisfying ministry within the heart of the believer.' For as the Word of God, in the power of the Spirit of God, takes effect in our lives (mind, heart, soul, conscience, will) a response is, of necessity, drawn out. People speak of reserving their position or withholding their judgement. But we cannot do that with God's Word, however much we might want to, or try to. It demands a response. There is, as it were, an RSVP attached to it which will not allow the luxury of 'no answer'.

What should be the response of the true Christian to God's Word?

1. Trembling at God's Word

'Rulers persecute me without cause, but my heart trembles at your word' (v.161). We do not hear too much of believers trembling these days, which is our loss. There is certainly all too little of trembling at God's Word. We tend, rather, to find it being taken lightly, preached only briefly, or, worse still, dramatized, mimed and made into entertainment. Surely all of this is guaranteed to call down the judgement of God upon His church, and maybe we are already seeing something of that. Where is the trembling? Where is the seriousness? Where is the awe? Where is the godly fear? One of the most important texts in the whole of the Bible, which has so much to teach about Christian worship, Christian life, and everything pertaining to Christianity, is Psalm 2:11: 'Serve the Lord with fear and rejoice with trembling.'

Here is Matthew Henry's comment on verse 161 of our psalm: 'Every gracious soul stands in awe of the Word of God, of the authority of its precepts and the terror of its threatenings; and to those that do so nothing appears, in the power and wrath of man, at all formidable.' He adds, 'The heart that stands in awe of God's Word is armed against the temptations that arise from persecution.'

Putting it another way, we may say that the Word of God makes our hearts quake and tremble because of its purity and power. You just cannot read it or have it preached to you and be left unaffected — even if, sometimes, it appears that way. This trembling and awe at God's Word arises in our souls because of our trembling and awe at God Himself — His 'endless wisdom, boundless power and awful purity'. We dread sinning against our gracious God. We dread grieving our loving heavenly Father. Consequently we dread disregarding or having an unfeeling conscience towards His Word, His law, His gospel and His providences. This is not slavish or legal fear; it is rather the freedom of the children of God. But, if we are really truthful, how much do we know of it?

2. Rejoicing in God's Word

The verse we have just quoted (Psalm 2:11) links together rejoicing and trembling. That is one of the reasons why it is such a key verse; yet it is often overlooked, with the result that so many contemporary Christians fail to see the connection between these two things. (Many even go further and regard them as foes!) But the believer who most trembles at

God's Word will be the one who most rejoices in it. Yes, he will! And his testimony will be: 'I rejoice in your promise like one who finds great spoil' (v.162). Let us agree wholeheartedly with Spurgeon when he says, 'It is a blessed thing to reverence the Word and to have an intense joy in it,' and when he adds, 'May we all know what the mixed emotion means.' He is right, too, when he continues: 'I will go the length of saying that unless we do have deep awe of the Word we shall never have high joy over it. Our rejoicing will be measured by our reverencing.'

Once more, our rejoicing in God's Word arises directly from our rejoicing in God Himself. His Word declares all that He has done for us, how He thinks about us and what He has prepared for us. There is a certain sense in which the Christian life is a blessed adventure of discovering more and more in God's Word of all the divine actions, thoughts, blessings and promises that relate to us and arise from God's rich and abundant grace.

3. Loving God's Word

If any theme has been explored with a blessed fulness in this psalm already, then it is this one! But it is so important that he mentions it again here. There are some things to do with the Christian life which you cannot say too often. They need to be underlined continually. And this tremendously important facet of the psalm's whole subject — loving God's Word — is one of those things. It bears repeating that it is not possible (truly and with a clear conscience) to say that you love the Lord if you do not love and prize His Word. We love Him because He first loved us, and loving Him, we love everything about Him; and that has to include His Word! So the psalmist is not afraid of being accused of repetition when he says, in verse 163, 'I hate and abhor falsehood, but I love your law.' He is consistent at this point. Are we?

4. Praising God for His Word

Verse 164 is a lovely verse: 'Seven times a day I praise you for your righteous laws.'

Horatius Bonar wrote,

> Fill Thou my life, O Lord my God,
> In every part with praise,
> That my whole being may proclaim
> Thy being and Thy ways.
>
> Not for the lip of praise alone,
> Nor e'en the praising heart,
> I ask, but for a life made up
> Of praise in every part.

That is exactly what the psalmist testifies to here — 'a life made up of praise in every part'. Some say that the phrase 'seven times a day' is to be taken literally, as a reference to stated times and seasons of prayer (both in private and in public). That may be so, but I am far rather inclined (with William Gurnall) to take this as the psalmist's way of expressing his habitual occupation in, and with, the praise of God. It was for him (and it should be for us) a duty without limits, whether in the morning, at mealtimes, as we go about our business, whenever we become particularly conscious of God's mercies throughout the day, in the secret place, with our families, in the church, in the evening, during the night — at any time at all, and at all times! Praise belongs to God. 'Great is the Lord, and most worthy of praise' (Psalm 48:1). We cannot praise Him either too much or too often. And the Word of God will act both as an incentive for our praising God and as one of His particular gifts, for which we give Him our heartfelt praise.

5. Possessing peace from God's Word

Here is another string worth plucking! 'Great peace have they who love your law, and nothing can make them stumble' (v.165). Peace is one of the richest themes of Scripture, whether we mean God's gracious gift of peace with Him described in Romans 5:1, or the spiritual blessing deep down within our souls of the peace of God spoken of in Philippians 4:7. Our God is 'the God of peace' (Romans 15:33), and Paul's prayer for the Thessalonians is this: 'Now may the Lord of peace himself give you peace at all times and in every way' (2 Thessalonians 3:16).

There is no word quite like this word 'peace'. It sums up the happiness, blessedness and eternal prosperity of the child of God, and it is related to God's Word. It was the Word (in the power of the Spirit) that first exposed our false peace, when we were not Christians, and that laid open for us the sole ground of peace for the sinner: Christ 'himself is our peace' (Ephesians 2:14). It continues to be the Word, as it is applied to us by the Spirit, through which God is pleased to bless us with His peace. 'You [God] will keep in perfect peace him whose mind is steadfast [AV, stayed on thee], because he trusts in you' (Isaiah 26:3). Any genuine treatment of the believer's response to God's Word must include reference to the 'great peace' which belongs to those who love His law, and as a result of which 'Nothing can make them stumble' — not even death itself!

This section of the psalm closes with two aspects of the theme which have already become very familiar to us as we have kept company with the psalmist: *hoping in*, or waiting for, *God's Word* and *obeying God's Word*.

Pause for a moment and meditate on the verbs used in verses 166-168: 'I wait . . . I follow . . . I obey'. If you were pressed, could you say with real honesty that the psalmist's full-orbed response to God's Word is yours too? What is your reply to the RSVP that is given in this section?

'May my cry come before you, O Lord;
  give me understanding according to your word.
May my supplication come before you;
  deliver me according to your promise.
May my lips overflow with praise,
  for you teach me your decrees.
May my tongue sing of your word,
  for all your commands are righteous.
May your hand be ready to help me,
  for I have chosen your precepts.
I long for your salvation, O Lord,
  and your law is my delight.
Let me live that I may praise you,
  and may your laws sustain me.
I have strayed like a lost sheep.
  Seek your servant,
  for I have not forgotten your commands'
                              (Psalm 119:169-176).

22.
Back home

Psalm 119:169-176

'I have strayed like a lost sheep. Seek your servant, for I have not forgotten your commands' (v.176).

One of the most exquisite, meaningful and moving pictures which the Bible gives of the unbeliever is that of the lost sheep. If you are not a Christian you are a lost sheep. You are away from the fold. You have broken through the hedge and bounds of God's commandments. You have gone astray into the paths of error and sin. You have forsaken the Shepherd of your soul.

> There were ninety and nine that safely lay
> In the shelter of the fold;
> But one was out on the hills away,
> Far off from the gates of gold,
> Away on the mountains wild and bare,
> Away from the tender Shepherd's care.
>
> (Elizabeth C. Clephane).

There is no picture which expresses quite so well the ideas of lostness, vulnerability and being in a condition of great danger as that of a sheep that has got lost. All of this gives rise in Scripture to the magnificent expressions of the Shepherd's love for the sheep, His search for the sheep, His joy over finding the sheep and His devoted care of the sheep.

Let us think for a moment of the parable told by the Lord Jesus Christ in Luke 15: 'Suppose one of you has a hundred sheep and loses one of them. Does he not leave the ninety-nine in the open country and go after the lost sheep until he finds it? And when he finds it, he joyfully puts it on his shoulders and goes home. Then he calls his friends and neighbours together and says, "Rejoice with me; I have found my lost sheep." I tell you that in the same way there will be more rejoicing in heaven over one sinner who repents than over ninety-nine righteous persons who do not need to repent.' That simple story, of course, sets forth the ministry of Christ Himself, the Shepherd of the sheep, towards those sinners He came to save. It is a picture that is matchless for beauty, tenderness and strength, just as He Himself is matchless for these things. What a glory it is to have such a wonderful Saviour and Shepherd!

Similarly, one of the most exquisite, meaningful and moving pictures in the Bible of the believer is that of the straying, or wandering, sheep. If you are a Christian you are one of Christ's sheep. This is a condition in which you remain secure by the grace of God that saved you, is keeping you and will present you faultless in heaven. The Shepherd Himself has promised concerning His sheep: 'I give them eternal life, and they shall never perish; no one can snatch them out of my hand' (John 10:28). But, sad to say, you will sometimes be a straying sheep. Why we should ever want to stray from such a Shepherd is amazing, but the fact is that at times we all do. We once were lost sheep. Grace has made us found sheep. But, sadly, we are all too often and all too easily straying sheep.

The psalmist has really come full circle. Do you recall the thrust of his testimony at the very beginning of the psalm? He acknowledged (from experience — he had not just got it from a textbook):

'Blessed are they whose ways are blameless,
    who walk according to the law of the Lord.
Blessed are they who keep his statutes
    and seek him with all their heart.'
Yet his testimony as he signs off in the very last verse of
    the psalm is:

'I have strayed like a lost sheep.
    Seek your servant . . .'

What has happened? The fact is that the psalmist knows his own heart. And surely we know ours too (or at least we should do), and we have to make the same hard and frank admissions. Even after our loftiest flights of devotion, our sincerest professions of faithfulness and our grandest declarations of love to God's Word and obedience to it, we have to come back (not once only, but time after time) to this sad, but honest and necessary, confession: 'I have strayed like a lost sheep.' That is what the psalmist does. That, surely, is what we must do too.

> Oh, to grace how great a debtor
> Daily I'm constrained to be!
> Let that grace, Lord, like a fetter,
> Bind my wandering heart to Thee.
> Prone to wander, Lord, I feel it,
> Prone to leave the God I love;
> Here's my heart, Lord; take and seal it,
> Seal it from Thy courts above!
>
> (Robert Robinson).

So the theme of this final section of the psalm is that of the straying believer returning to God's Word, having wandered all over the place and having fallen (actually or potentially) into all manner of trouble. Isn't this an alarmingly accurate picture of every one of us who truly belongs to the Lord?

Glancing through this section verse by verse, it is possible to discern areas into which either the psalmist himself had fallen, or into which there is a real danger that we might wander off and fall in the Christian life.

Let me pick out a few of these and urge you to apply them to your own heart, with self-examination and prayer.

1. The danger of straying into folly (v.169)

The psalmist utters a fresh cry for understanding, wisdom and right judgement — which must always be that which is 'according to your word'. We are in continual need as Christians of having our mind and all our thoughts made captive to that faultless Word of God, in order that we may be kept from rushing off on foolish impulses of our own, or following the often sinful or selfish desires of our unmortified hearts.

2. The danger of straying into trouble (v.170)

This time he utters an earnest supplication for deliverance and help, 'according to [God's] promise'. 'With the difficulty,' he is saying, 'please provide the way of escape. In the extremity, please send your support.' It is no use our relying on our own strength, or trusting in our own ingenuity, to deliver ourselves. We can get into trouble easily enough on our own, but we need one mightier than ourselves to deliver us.

3. The danger of straying into ingratitude (v.171)

Only in the previous section (v.165) the psalmist spoke of the believer's happy duty of praising God, and here his plea before the Lord is: 'May my lips overflow with praise.' What a lovely picture that is — lips overflowing with praise to God! Matthew Henry comments that 'We have learned nothing to purpose if we have not learned to praise God.' And Charles Bridges remarks, 'How happy it is to bring to God a heart as large in praise as in prayer.' But do we? Are there not a whole host of tokens of God's grace, favour, goodness, providence and such like which are still lying 'hidden in unthankfulness' and without praise? Our slowness to praise God, our unwillingness to praise Him and our forgetfulness in praising Him should lie more heavily upon our consciences than is usually the case.

4. The danger of straying into silence (v.172)

'May my tongue sing [or speak] of your word, for all your commands are righteous.' It is very important to make God's Word both the governor and the subject matter of our conversation, and to testify from the Word (and the Word known through experience) to the righteousness and faithfulness of

God. Those who walk in fellowship with the Lord will not be
without a fresh and continuing testimony to the Lord. We are
not to be dumb creatures. In this connection we remember
the apostle Peter's exhortation: 'But in your hearts set apart
Christ as Lord. Always be prepared to give an answer to
everyone who asks you to give the reason for the hope that
you have. But do this with gentleness and respect, keeping a
clear conscience, so that those who speak maliciously against
your good behaviour in Christ may be ashamed of their slander' (1 Peter 3:15-16).

5. The danger of straying into self-reliance and self sufficiency (v.173)

In his request, 'May your hand be ready to help me,' the
psalmist demonstrates his felt need for God's comforting,
supporting and supplying aid, without which we cannot continue to stand. The arm of flesh (our own or anyone else's)
will fail us. Only God's arm is to be relied upon. There is
nothing as incongruous as a self-reliant Christian!

6. The danger of straying into coldness (v.174)

The note of longing surfaces once more: 'I long for your salvation, O Lord, and your law is my delight.' The psalmist's
desires for the stirring, quickening influences of God have
been one of the threads running right through the psalm. How
we need the Lord to warm us up and keep us warm! We
must never be satisfied with being in a cold, or lukewarm,
condition.

7. The danger of straying into worldliness (v.175)

For whom do you live? 'Let me live that I may praise you, and
may your laws sustain me,' prays the psalmist. Though conscious of having wandered and strayed, he longs again to live
for God and for eternity. Oh, that we might be granted a fresh
desire and renewed vigour to that same holy end!

So here we are at the end of the psalm. Again and again we have found ourselves mirrored here, in all the 'ups and downs', 'in and outs' and 'ons and offs' of Christian experience, including this last one — that of being straying sheep. What is the way back? Acknowledging that we have wandered; confessing our sin and failure before God, without any excusing of ourselves; coming in godly sorrow and true repentance to Him at His throne of grace, and pleading fresh mercies in Jesus' name. Such will continue to be our experience as life goes on, until that blessed day when He takes us to Himself in the glory that He has prepared, where, at last, there will be no more sinning and no more need for repentance!

I have several times quoted from David Dickson, a Scottish minister of an earlier century. It is appropriate to conclude this short study of Psalm 119 with the memorable words he spoke as the end of his earthly pilgrimage drew near, for with this precious psalm still ringing in our ears (and, better still, lodging in our minds and hearts) this needs to be *our* daily testimony as those who, by God's grace, would seek to 'walk according to the law of the Lord,' even though we so often appear to be straying sheep along the way. This is what he said: 'I have taken all my good deeds and all my bad, and cast them in a heap before the Lord, and fled from both, and betaken myself to the Lord Jesus Christ, and in Him I have sweet peace.'

Bibliography

Choice volumes on Psalm 119

Bridges, Charles. *Psalm 119,* Banner of Truth Trust.
Campbell, Murdoch. *From Grace to Glory,* Banner of Truth Trust.
Dickson, David. *The Psalms,* Banner of Truth Trust.
Henry, Matthew, *Commentary on the Whole Bible,* vol. 3, MacDonald.
Miller, J. Graham. *The Treasury of His Promises,* Banner of Truth Trust.
Plumer, W. S. *Psalms,* Banner of Truth Trust.
Preacher's Complete Homiletic Commentary, vol. 12, Baker Book House.
Spurgeon, C. H. *The Treasury of David,* vol. 6, Evangelical Press.

Other works quoted in the text

Appéré, Guy. *Dialogue with God,* Evangelical Press.
Bolton, Samuel. *The True Bounds of Christian Freedom,* Banner of Truth Trust.
Brooks, Thomas. *Works,* vol. 2, Banner of Truth Trust.
Henry, Matthew. *Directions for Daily Communion with God,* Evangelical Press.
MacDonald, Donald. *Christian Experience,* Banner of Truth Trust.
Pink, A. W. *Profiting from the Word,* Banner of Truth Trust.
Rutherford, Samuel. *Letters,* Banner of Truth Trust.